What Will We Play Today?

Drama, Movement and Music Arts Games for Children Aged 0–5 Years

Veronicah Larkin and Louie Suthers

 **Brilliant Publications**

Publisher's Information

Published by:
>   Brilliant Publications
>   1 Church View
>   Sparrow Hall Farm
>   Edlesborough
>   Dunstable
>   LU6 2ES

Tel: **01525 229720**
Fax: **01525 229725**
Website: **www.brilliantpublications.co.uk**
E-mail: **sales@brilliantpublications.co.uk**

Written by Veronica Larkin and Louie Suthers
Illustrated by Jan Wade

Originally published in 1995 by Pademelon Press., 7/10 Anella Avenue, Castle Hill, New South Wales, 2154 Australia

© Veronicah Larkin and Louie Suthers.

ISBN 1 897675 739

First published in the UK in 2000, reprinted in 2002
10 9 8 7 6 5 4 3 2

Printed in Malta by Interprint Ltd.

This book contains fun games based on drama, movement and music. Many of the games can be readily adadpted to provide increased challenges as children grow and develop.

Preface

As far back as we can remember, we have played games. We like to think that while pre-historic men and women were busily inventing the wheel, pre-historic children were just as busily playing games. When we observe young children at play it's easy to conclude that they look upon the process in much the same way that we would look upon breathing or eating, not so much a choice but an essential life-sustaining experience. The commitment and the passion that young children bring to playing games is compelling and fascinating, and has been an important inspiration for this book.

Some people collect model cars, stamps from exotic destinations or priceless works of art – we just happen to collect games. Over many years, we have begged, borrowed, overheard, adapted, modified and devised literally hundreds of games suitable for young children. Some of these games were taught to us by adults and some by children. Other games we stumbled upon by accident (a spare few minutes, a group of eager children, a stray scarf – suddenly a game emerged.)

Sometimes a game half-remembered became a new game or a game half-liked was adapted to become a better game. There were other times when a sudden rainstorm would bring the children indoors and a spontaneous new game appeared through necessity. Other times a game emerges to settle excited children during an outing, to comfort an anxious child separating from mum or dad, to affirm a shy or withdrawn child or to celebrate a child's birthday. As our games selection continued to grow, an important fact emerged: all our games emphasized drama, movement and music, so we created a term for the kinds of games we love to collect and play: *arts games*.

During the years that we have been sharing our art games with undergraduate teaching students, pre-school personnel, academics and families of young children, we have grown accustomed to hearing the lament that our games were not available in printed form. Frequently we have found ourselves singing the songs over the telephone and explaining the games via letters and fax; we've been approached at conferences, on campus, in libraries and even in the supermarket by pre-school personnel who have attended one of our workshops but 'can't quite remember how Action Rap goes ...'. It became increasingly clear to us that publishing a collection of our games would be a useful endeavour, and so this book was finally born.

We would like to express our gratitude to the many individuals and organizations who have assisted us in the research, trialling, editing and publication of this book. We acknowledge our academic colleagues for their valuable guidance, support and encouragement.

Written by Veronicah Larkin and Louie Suthers
www.brilliantpublications.co.uk

Introduction

Play is a critical element in the healthy development of young children. When children play they make sense of the world around them. Play can be demanding, challenging, exacting, sometimes frustrating and frequently very rewarding. Young children's physical, cognitive, social, emotional and creative development can be richly enhanced by quality play experiences. Sometimes children's play is entirely spontaneous, imaginative and free, without a role for any adult. In other situations adults may guide or initiate play experiences for children. Adults who work with young children are always on the lookout for new ideas, content and strategies to assist them in facilitating high-quality play activities. Games, in their many forms, should have a developmental approach, offering a challenging and highly enjoyable way of providing guided play experiences for young children.

Art games are games based on drama, movement or music, or a combination of these. Usually an adult will initiate and guide the game playing. The games may be played by one adult and one child or by several adults and a group of children. Throughout the book we have offered a suggested group size for each game.

It may be said that a good game is one that 'grows' with the children. You may find that many of the games become firm favourites and are requested by children over and over again. They can be readily adapted to provide additional elements or increased challenges as children grow and develop their own abilities and skills. However, this is only a suggestion of ages, as we have seen some of our toddler games cleverly modified to become appropriately challenging experiences for four and five year olds. With a little thought and imaginative planning, children don't have to automatically 'grow out' of their favourite games.

Many of the games in this book do not require any materials, resources or equipment. Others require resources which are available in most homes or pre-school settings. Resources such as balls, hoops, ropes, sticks and sound makers are easily purchased or made and none require substantial financial outlay. Importantly, none of the resources used in our games are difficult to transport or store and many can be used

in a variety of different games. A small number of games require specific pieces of equipment, so we have provided simple instructions for making these yourself with minimum fuss and expense.

For some people playing games in a pre-school setting is associated with formal group time, where an adult sits on a chair and the children are seated on a mat. While some of our games can certainly be played in this manner, others can be played in a wide variety of contexts. Many of the games can be played in both indoor and outdoor environments, according to the weather and your available space and resources. We have played our games under a variety of different circumstances; for example, while rocking a baby to sleep; on a change table; in the bath; on the bus; on an outing; gathered around the water trough or play-dough table; in the sand pit, in the home corner and under a shady tree in the local park. Naturally, as in all children's activities, these games require careful adult supervision to ensure the safety and well-being of the children involved. Additionally, many of the games can be played as part of regular care-giving routines and as transition experiences. Some of the games have also been very successful at children's parties and other festivities.

The games we have collected for this book are deliberately non-competitive. There is a strong emphasis on the process of playing rather than on winning. We believe that playing games encourages children to share, take turns, co-operate, listen, respond and accept the contributions of the other children. Games that are solely based on winning, elimination or overt comparison of skills have been excluded from this collection in favour of games which offer opportunities for children to operate at their own pace. An effective game is one that encourages a variety of responses and levels of participation. Consequently, many of our games include suggestions for simple modifications which may be useful when working with children who have special needs. Issues related to tolerance and inclusion, such as those promoted by an anti-bias

Written by Veronicah Larkin and Louie Suthers
www.brilliantpublications.co.uk

Introduction

curriculum are highlighted. We have included a number of our favourite games with languages other than English. Playing these games may encourage children to accept and value a variety of cultures and traditions.

Many adults working in pre-school settings express concern over the appropriateness of children rehearsing and presenting a performance for families on open days, family nights or the annual Christmas concert. As an enjoyable and developmentally suitable alternative, you might consider encouraging families and friends to share in a selection of art games with the children. Naturally, you can invite your audience to become participants in the games as well. Recently we had the pleasure of attending a local pre-school's 'Grandparents' morning' and were delighted to see an enthusiastic and energetic group of older people volunteering to join their grand-children as they crawled under and over ropes.

Pre-schools, nursery schools and other organizations involved in fund raising, might like to substitute the traditional 'games night' for an 'art games night'. Experience has shown us that a quick game of *Musical Hoops* is an excellent ice-breaker for newly introduced adults at these gatherings. Many of the games in this collection can be readily adapted for adults playing and are certain to liven up your next fund-raising event, inset day or committee meeting!

Often when you introduce a new game to a group you follow the 'rules' very closely. You may find that you play these games exactly as we have suggested. However, be assured that we love nothing more than to see our games modified to suit individual tastes, skills, confidence levels and interests. Frequently we have included variations at the end of a game to enable you to expand or extend it. With a little experience you may find yourself adding variations to games or inventing your own games from scratch. We certainly hope that you will look upon this book as a starting point to stimulate your thinking, planning and teaching, and not just as a

finished product. Sometimes people tell us they would like to include more arts experiences in their programme but feel they lack the confidence or resources to do so. Our views on this matter are very simple ... the essential quality for effective arts teaching in early childhood has very little to do with talent and almost everything to do with enthusiasm. If you have been reluctant to engage in dramatic play, movement or music with young children, now is the time to recognize your great talent for enthusiasm and consider the endless possibilities that arts games may provide for you and your children.

It is important to remember that some of the games require high levels of active participation from you. If it has been a while since you've engaged in any energetic movement or dancing, take things slowly at first. Gradually and safely work up to it and don't overdo things. We'd hate to think that our arts games led to aches and sprains!

Finally, all the games in this collection have been extensively trialled with adults and children in a variety of settings. Adults' and children's responses were carefully noted and games were eliminated or changed, based on these observations. However, we are always open to suggestions and feedback so if you have any ideas on ways we could improve any of the games in this collection we would love to hear from you.

Let the games begin!

Contents

Written by Veronicah Larkin and Louie Suthers

www.brilliantpublications.co.uk

Contents

Game	Babies	Toddlers	3–5 years	Page no.
Make a cake	●	●		46
Mal mal			●	47
Manual road			●	48
Match the shakers		●	●	49
Mother and Father and Uncle John	●	●		50
Mr Eddy had a teddy		●	●	51
Musical hoops		●	●	52
My little hen (Mi Gallinita)			●	53
Newspaper game		●	●	54
Obwisana			●	55
One in the middle		●	●	56
One two		●	●	57
Over the stones	●	●		58
Pass the shaker		●	●	59
Peek-a-boo	●	●		60
People skittles			●	61
Person obstacle course		●	●	62
Pizza, sausage	●	●		63
Polly whoops!	●	●		64
Rattle snake			●	65
Ride baby ride	●	●		66
Ring-a-ring-a-rosie		●	●	67
Roll that big ball		●	●	68
Roll the ball	●	●		69
Round Australia			●	70
Sandy girl		●	●	71
Shopping spree			●	72
Snakey rope		●	●	73
Sound moves		●	●	74
Spot the difference		●	●	75
Sqeeze the ball and pass it on		●	●	76
Stop and go		●	●	77
Swinging	●	●		78
Tap your shoulders	●	●	●	79
Teddy sing a song		●	●	80

Contents

Written by Veronicah Larkin and Louie Suthers
www.brilliantpublications.co.uk

Age:	birth–5 years
Grouping:	individual/small/medium/large groups, babies – knee-bouncing game, older children – informally gathered around an adult
Resources:	none

A ram sam sam
A singing game

How to play

- Knee-bouncing game: hold baby on knee facing you and sing song. On 'a ram sam sam' bounce baby up and down; on 'guli guli' gently rock baby from side to side; 'arafi' lower carefully backwards. With young babies, ensure firm head support throughout.
- Action game: sing song and add the following actions; 'a ram sam sam' jump up and down; 'guli guli' shake all over; on 'arafi' stretch up high and touch the ground.
- Encourage children to invent their own alternative actions.

Variations

- Older, more experienced children can play it as a circle game. Encourage them to devise movements or actions they can do as they walk around in a circle.

Written by Veronicah Larkin and Louie Suthers
www.brilliantpublications.co.uk

What will we play today?

Action rap
A following game

How to play

☐ The verse is a 4-line echo rap; leader chants a line with matching actions then everyone imitates the words and the actions. Everyone joins in the song and actions for the chorus. The chorus is sung twice.

Variations

☐ Encourage the children to invent other verses. It doesn't matter at all if they don't rhyme. Having 4 children contribute a line each works well.

Age:	4–5 years
Grouping:	small/medium/large group, in own space with room to move, children facing an adult/leader
Resources:	none

Chorus   L.S.

Ev' ry bo – dy clap, clap, clap, Let's all do the Act – ion rap.

Action Rap

1. We shake our hands   *Echo:*   (We shake our hands)
   We stamp our feet   (We stamp our feet)
   We knock our knees   (We knock our knees)
   And we clap the beat.   (And we clap the beat).

Chorus

2. We twirl our arms   *Echo:*   (We twirl our arms)
   We swing our hips   (We swing our hips)
   We shrug our shoulders   (We shrug our shoulders)
   And we kiss our lips.   (X X X) = kissing sounds

Chorus

3. We stretch up high   *Echo:*   (We stretch up high)
   We touch the ground   (We touch the ground)
   We roll our hands   (We roll our hands)
   And we spin around.   (And we spin around).

Chorus

Written by Veronicah Larkin and Louie Suthers
www.brilliantpublications.co.uk

Age:	birth–18 months
Grouping:	individual, holding or nursing the child on your lap or seated next to the child on the floor
Resources:	none

Baby Beth

An action game

How to play

- ◘ Hold the child safely in your arms. As you say the rhyme gently move the child according to the actions.
- ◘ Repeat while child remains interested.
- ◘ You can substitute the child's own name in place of 'Beth'.

Variations

- ◘ According to the child's age/experience you can invent new actions and new nonsense words to match.

Rhyme

Riggle, raggle, roggle, ree
Baby Beth can roll to me
Biggle, baggle, boggle, bee
Baby Beth can bounce to me
Jiggle, jaggle, joggle, jee
Baby Beth can jump to me
Figgle, faggle, foggle, fee
Baby Beth can fly to me.

Written by Veronicah Larkin and Louie Suthers
www.brilliantpublications.co.uk

What will we play today?

Balloon tennis

A passing game

Age:	2–5 years
Grouping:	small/medium group
Resources:	1 inflated balloon for every 2 children

How to play

- ◻ Invite children to stand opposite their partners and to pass the balloon gently back and forth.
- ◻ Children might begin by using their hands and later move on to moving the balloon with their heads/feet/other body parts as appropriate.
- ◻ As children become more experienced the distance between partners may be increased, or divided by a stretched out rope. The children can move the balloon over or under the rope.
- ◻ You might encourage the children to try to keep the balloon in the air and avoid allowing it to fall onto the floor.
- ◻ Hospitalized children have been known to play this game for extended periods of time by inventing a range of new ways to move the balloon from one bed to the next.

Variations

- ◻ Older/more experienced children can move the balloon to a pre-arranged point in the room by using their chins, foreheads, backs, bottoms, tummies or whatever else the children suggest. It's important to keep in mind that when a balloon bursts you need to clear away all the pieces as young children have been known to swallow and choke on balloon remnants. You might like to substitute a soft rubber or plastic ball for the balloon in these games.

12
What will we play today?

Written by Veronicah Larkin and Louie Suthers
www.brilliantpublications.co.uk

Age:	2–5 years
Grouping:	small/middle/large group, standing in a circle.
Resources:	none

Birthday candle game

A drama game

This game is ideal to play on a child's birthday.

How to play

◻ Children stand in a circle, holding each other's hands, to represent a round birthday cake.

◻ Invite a number of children to stand in the middle of the circle, to represent birthday candles. The number will depend upon the age of the 'birthday child'.

◻ As the rhyme is said, the 'birthday child' moves amongst the 'candles' and blows on each, causing them to fall over. (In the interest of hygiene you might encourage the child to simply pretend to blow on the other children.)

◻ In the rhyme, use the birthday child's age and name.

Rhyme

Craig is having a birthday
And he is three today
See him blow the candles out
Hooray! Hooray! Hooray!

Chook chook

A singing game

How to play
- ☐ Sing the song and clap the beat.
- ☐ Keep the beat on the floor or knees. Encourage the children to suggest other body parts to tap.
- ☐ Some children can be 'chooks', walking about, scratching and flapping their wings as others sing.
- ☐ Repeat as many times as required.

Variations
- ☐ Use sticks to tap the beat of the song.

Note
Chook chook is a traditional Australian Aboriginal children's song.

Chook chook padulu wanari wita means 'chicken with the small thigh'.

Age:	2¹/₂–5 years
Grouping:	small/medium/large group, informally gathered around an adult
Resources:	none (optional sticks)

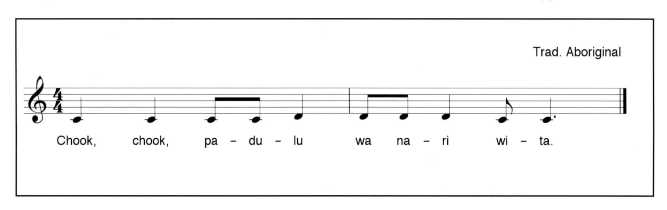

Trad. Aboriginal

Chook, chook, pa – du – lu wa na – ri wi – ta.

Written by Veronicah Larkin and Louie Suthers
www.brilliantpublications.co.uk

Age:	3–5 years
Grouping:	small/medium group, children make train formations with 3 or 4 children in each train, hoops are placed on the floor as stations.
Resources:	hoops

Chuff choof

A hoop game

How to play

- Sing song as children chuff around the room. At the end of the song, trains stop at a station and passengers may leave or join any train. Repeat the song as many times as required. You may like to swap engines from time to time.

Variations

- Start with only engines (single children) and everyone else waiting at stations. Engines frequently like to make steam train sounds as they make their journey.
- Change the speed of the song; trains can accordingly get faster or slower.
- Play the game in an outdoor environment using trees, trestles, traffic cones or similar, as stations.
- Non-mobile children enjoy this song as a knee-bouncing or lap game. A pushchair can also become a train for this game.

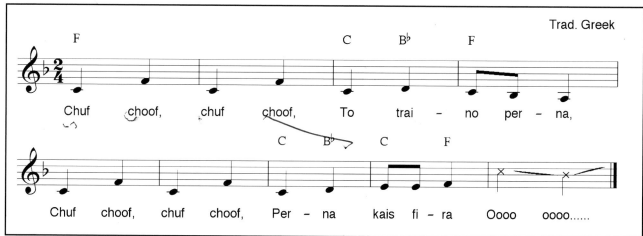

Come on and clap

A movement game

How to play

- Sing the song and clap. Repeat. With children under 3 years it is important to repeat each verse as many younger children take some time to join in. If you don't repeat each action, some of the toddlers will only just have started to participate as you change to a new action.
- Change the action and the words. Swaying, bouncing, shaking and jumping are effective with toddlers. Older children may like to suggest more adventurous actions like twisting, crawling, rolling, twirling or galloping.
- Try as many different actions as you wish.

Age:	20 months–4 years
Grouping:	small/medium group, younger children can play this game gathered around an adult; older so more experienced children can use a circle formation
Resources:	none

Variations

- Encourage children to suggest actions. Some 3- and 4- year-olds will be able to name their actions, but with younger children you'll need to label the action and substitute appropriate words in the song.
- Many children will focus on the physical activity rather than on the singing. While you may like to commend children who are singing and moving, be assured that when they are ready and able to do both, children will. Generally older children will be better able to do two things at once than younger ones.

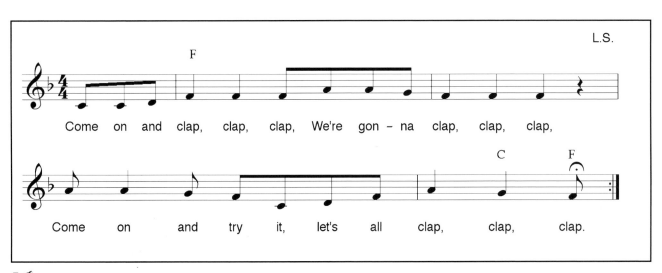

Written by Veronicah Larkin and Louie Suthers

www.brilliantpublications.co.uk

Age:	4–5 years
Grouping:	small/medium/large group, seated in a circle
Resources:	a pair of sticks for each player

Cool drummer
A stick game

How to play
- ❑ Everyone sings the song and taps their sticks on the floor to the beat.
- ❑ At the end of the song, everyone stops and the leader taps a short pattern. Everyone echoes the pattern.
- ❑ Repeat the game as many times as appropriate.

Variations
- ❑ Let children take turns in being the leader. This not only keeps children actively involved but also encourages creative expression. Don't worry if the patterns are of varying lengths and complexities.
- ❑ Patterns to be copied may be tapped or played on the floor or in any other ways the children devise.

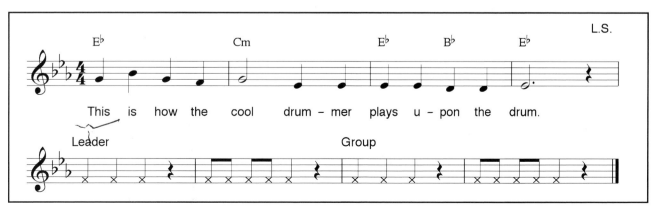

This is how the cool drum – mer plays u – pon the drum.

Leader   Group

Dressed to thrill

A singing game

Tune: Here we go round the mulberry bush

Age:	3–5 years
Grouping:	small/medium group, children gathered informally around an adult
Resources:	a wide collection of easy pull-on clothes such as pyjamas, track suits, t-shirts; an assortment of accessories such as socks, shoes, hats, scarves, shawls, ties, bags, sunglasses, gloves; 4 hoops or 4 cardboard boxes.

How to play

- Place a bundle of clothes and accessories in each hoop/box. Ensure there is a variety in each.
- Invite four children to be the 'dressers'.
- As the children are singing the song through several times the four 'dressers' try to put on as many clothes and accessories as possible.
- Provide an opportunity for other interested children to have a turn at being a 'dresser'.
- Physically challenged children, who may have difficulty dressing themselves, can be assisted by another child or adult.

Variations

- This game does not have to be played as a competitive race, and the child wearing the most clothes need not be described as the winner.

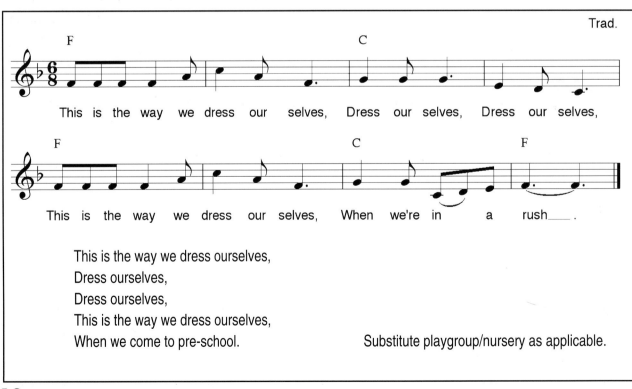

This is the way we dress ourselves,
Dress ourselves,
Dress ourselves,
This is the way we dress ourselves,
When we come to pre-school.

Substitute playgroup/nursery as applicable.

Written by Veronicah Larkin and Louie Suthers
www.brilliantpublications.co.uk

Age:	3–5 years
Grouping:	small/medium group, children gathered informally around an adult
Resources:	a set of cardboard oval shapes, each a different colour, to represent Easter eggs.

Easter bunny fun

A singing game

Tune: **Everybody do this**

How to play

- ◻ Spread the Easter eggs out on a mat and encourage children to examine them carefully.
- ◻ Invite a child to play the role of the Easter Bunny.
- ◻ The remaining children close their eyes and sing the song while the Easter Bunny takes one Easter egg away.
- ◻ At the end of the song the children open their eyes and work out which egg is missing.
- ◻ The game continues with other interested children taking turns of playing the Easter Bunny.

Variations

- ◻ You might like to devise a simple costume for the child playing the role of the Easter Bunny. A set of floppy ears can be made by filling a pair of white socks with soft padding and attaching them to a white woolly hat. The Easter Bunny's tail can be made by attaching white cotton wool pieces onto the seat of an old pair of white pyjama or track suit bottoms.
- ◻ You could use real Easter eggs (either chocolate or dyed) in this game.

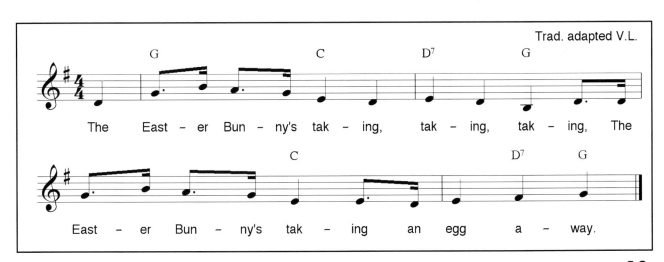

Trad. adapted V.L.

The East – er Bun – ny's tak – ing, tak – ing, tak – ing, The

East – er Bun – ny's tak – ing an egg a – way.

Epo e ti ti ai

A stick game

Age: 3–5 years
Grouping: small/medium/large group, seated in a circle
Resources: a pair of sticks for each player

How to play

- Sing the song and tap the beat on the ground with sticks. Repeat song and change the stick pattern each time. Try the following:
  – use alternate hands to tap the floor
  – cross and uncross hands
  – tap the floor and sticks together; alternatively
  – hold one stick still at waist height and use the other hand to alternately tap on the floor
  – tap floor and sticks alternately in a slow quick quick pattern (_ _ _ _ _ _ etc).

Variations

- As the song is repeated many times during the course of the game, children pick up the song quite quickly. There is no need to teach the words separately. Encourage the children to do the actions as well as sing the song.
- Children will invent other stick patterns to go with the song. These will become more complex as their skills increase.

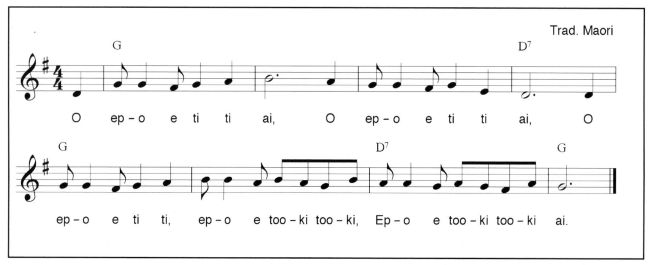

O ep-o e ti ti ai, O ep-o e ti ti ai, O ep-o e ti ti, ep-o e too-ki too-ki, Ep-o e too-ki too-ki ai.

Written by Veronicah Larkin and Louie Suthers
www.brilliantpublications.co.uk

Age:	1–5 years
Grouping:	small/large group circle, or sitting informally around an adult
Resources:	a pair of rhythm sticks for each player, older children may be able to achieve a similar effect with chop sticks

Everybody tap your sticks

A stick game
Tune: If you're happy and you know it

How to play

- ☐ Sing song and tap sticks.
- ☐ Encourage children to devise other actions with sticks, such as waving or banging the floor.
- ☐ Change the words of the song to match each new action. Older children will often label their action but you will have to name the suggestions for the younger ones.

Variations

Use the game with other known tunes, such as 'Here we go round the mulberry bush' or 'Everybody do this'. Don't be concerned if some children concentrate on their sticks rather than on singing the song. When children are able to manage both singing and tapping, they will.

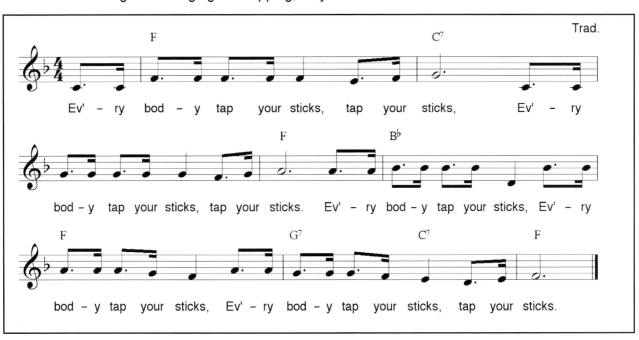

Trad.

Ev' – ry bod – y tap your sticks, tap your sticks, Ev' – ry bod – y tap your sticks, tap your sticks. Ev' – ry bod – y tap your sticks, Ev' – ry bod – y tap your sticks, Ev' – ry bod – y tap your sticks, Ev' – ry bod – y tap your sticks, tap your sticks.

Written by Veronicah Larkin and Louie Suthers
www.brilliantpublications.co.uk

Father is a butcher

A tickling game

How to play

This is a tickling game. Hold one of the child's hands. Say the rhyme and do the actions (below).

Age:	1–3 years
Grouping:	individual
Resources:	none

Variations

◻ Older children will enjoy reversing roles and 'doing the game' to you.

◻ Change the words to give parents different roles; such as 'Mother is a butcher, Father chops the meat ... '. Or include the names of other significant adults, such as family members, friends or carers.

Rhyme

Father is a butcher	*Clap the palm of child's hand.*
Mother chops the meat	*Chop the palm of child's hand.*
But I'm a little hot dog	*Tickle fingers up child's arm.*
Who runs around the street.	*Tickle fingers around child's neck.*

Written by Veronicah Larkin and Louie Suthers
www.brilliantpublications.co.uk

Age:	birth–2 years
Grouping:	individual, holding or nursing child
Resources:	a collection of differently textured objects/materials, such as a feather, wool, synthetic fur, satin, sponge, scrunched-up tissue paper, foam rubber.

Feather up feather down

A tickling game

How to play

- Hold the child in your arms.
- As you say the rhyme, gently pass the object/material over the child's skin (hands, arms, legs).

Variations

- Ensure that all materials selected are safe to make contact with the sensitive skin of a young child.
- This game can be successfully played with visually impaired babies and toddlers.

Rhyme

Feather up
Feather down
Feather tickles round and round.

Substitute name of material/object.

Find the colour

A movement game

Age: 4–5 years
Resources: recorded music, a large coloured mat (see details below)

How to play

- ◘ Spread out the colour mat in an open area.
- ◘ Invite the children to move/dance around the room while the music is playing.
- ◘ When the music stops name a colour and encourage the children to run and stand on that colour circle.
- ◘ Continue the game in this manner, choosing different colours each time the music stops.

Variations

- ◘ This is not a competitive game. Each colour circle should be of sufficient size to allow a number of children to stand on it comfortably, at the same time.
- ◘ For older/more experienced children you could add an additional challenge by inviting children to touch the colour circle with other body parts, such as 'put your hand on the green circle.'
- ◘ Children sometimes enjoy touching different colour circles with different body parts at the same time, such as 'put one foot on the yellow circle and one hand on the blue circle.'

How to make a colour mat

Choose a length of white calico or similar sturdy fabric, or even an old white tablecloth or cotton bedspread. The size will depend on the numbers of children playing and your available floor space, however, 2 metres x 2 metres is an appropriate guide.

Using a large round plate, trace approximately 12 circles randomly onto the fabric. The exact number of circles will depend on the size of the mat. Ensure there is sufficient space between the circles for children to move comfortably, however, the circles should be sufficiently close to each other so that children can touch 2 or more with different body parts at the same time.

Using a non-toxic long-lasting paint, colour each circle. You may prefer to limit yourself to the primary colours, or you may wish to add additional colours.

Spray-on fabric protector will help to preserve the mat's life.

Written by Veronicah Larkin and Louie Suthers
www.brilliantpublications.co.uk

Age:	4–5 years
Grouping:	small/medium group, large open floor space
Resources:	recorded music, a piece of white chalk

Find the shape
A movement game

How to play

- ◘ Using white chalk draw the outlines of 4 large shapes on the floor, one each of a square, rectangle, triangle and circle. The size of the outlines will be determined by the number of children playing the game.
- ◘ Encourage children to move/dance around the room while the music plays.
- ◘ When the music stops you can name a shape and encourage children to stand in that outline. This is not a competitive game as all children will be able to fit into the outline.
- ◘ The game can be repeated while children's interest is maintained.

Variations

- ◘ For older/more experienced children you can provide the additional challenge of simply holding up a shape card and encouraging children to look closely at the card. They will then stand in the corresponding outline.
- ◘ Other variations include statements such as 'stand on one foot in the circle shape' or jump over to the square shape.' These directions can be made increasingly more challenging depending upon the age/ experience of the children.
- ◘ You can assist mobility impaired children to invent other ways of locating and indicating the correct shape.

Note
White chalk is easily removed from carpet and other surfaces at the end of the game.

Written by Veronicah Larkin and Louie Suthers
www.brilliantpublications.co.uk

Five in the bed

An action game

How to play

- Sing song and perform these actions on the following words:

  five in the bed – *hold up the number of fingers*

  roll over – *roll hands in a circular motion*

  one fell out – *clap hands three times.*

- Continue in a similar way for four, three, two in the bed.

- Final verse:

  'There was one in the bed and the little one said 'goodnight'.

  On 'goodnight' do any appropriate sleeping action.

Variations

- Say the words as a rhyme rather than singing them. Many children aged 3 to 5 years are still learning to use their voices to sing. Alternating singing and chanting helps them differentiate between the two.

Age:	3–5 years
Grouping:	small/medium group
Resources:	none

- Older children may enjoy acting out the song with mattresses and blankets.

Trad.

There were five in the bed, And the litt – le one said 'roll ov – er, roll ov – er', So they all rolled ov – er and one fell out.

Written by Veronicah Larkin and Louie Suthers

www.brilliantpublications.co.uk

Age:	20 months–4 years
Grouping:	small/medium/large group, informally gathered around an adult, or in a circle with older children if appropriate
Resources:	none

Follow me
A following game

How to play

- ◻ Sing the song. The song has lots of repetition so there are several opportunities in each verse for young children to join in, either with the song or the actions.
- ◻ Encourage children to suggest alternative actions. Change the words accordingly.

Variations

- ◻ This game works well with a puppet as the leader (instructor).
- ◻ Older/more experienced children may want to have a turn as the leader.
- ◻ When the children know the game well, play it with two even groups rather than a leader and the group.
- ◻ Hold the last note of each line as the other group sings. This creates a reverberating effect like an echo.
- ◻ For pre-verbal children, or those with communication disorders, restrict the copying to actions and movements you know they can do.

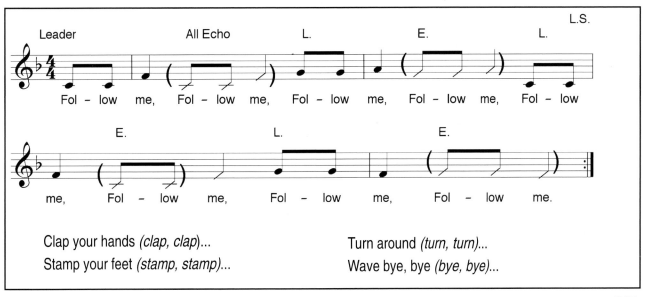

Clap your hands *(clap, clap)*...
Stamp your feet *(stamp, stamp)*...

Turn around *(turn, turn)*...
Wave bye, bye *(bye, bye)*...

Follow the sound

A listening game

Age:	2–5 years
Grouping:	small/medium/large group, large open space suitable for movement
Resources:	2 different musical instruments/sound makers, 2 adults

How to play

- ☐ Both adults should initially acquaint the children with the different sounds produced by each instrument.
- ☐ The 2 adults proceed to move around the room, alternately playing their instruments.
- ☐ Encourage the children to listen carefully to the sound and to follow behind the adult who is playing at the time.

Variations

- ☐ The adults may accompany their sound making with a simple action, such as nodding the head as the tambourine is shaken, or swaying from side to side as the bells are rung. As children follow the sound around the room they can also imitate the actions.
- ☐ For younger/less experienced children the two instruments should produce clearly different sounds to assist them in differentiating the sounds.

- ☐ As children become more experienced, two identical instruments can be used in this game, encouraging the children to listen carefully to the direction of the sounds.

Written by Veronicah Larkin and Louie Suthers
www.brilliantpublications.co.uk

Age:	4–5 years
Grouping:	small/medium/large group, small groups can gather informally around adult; for larger groups a circle can be used
Resources:	none

Getting dressed

An action game
Tune:
She'll be coming round the mountain

How to play

■ Sing the song and dramatize the actions.

■ Encourage children to make suggestions about what they might put on next and alter the words to suit. The game can have as many verses as required.

Variations

■ Play with real clothes from the dressing-up box.

■ Get dressed for an occasion that requires particular clothing or equipment, such as going to the beach or going out in the rain.

■ Invite one child to be observed and make the verses correspond to what he or she is wearing, for example 'We're putting on our green boots ... blue jeans ... black top ... just like Neryl.'

■ Play with dolls that can be dressed. Match the words to each doll's clothes, for example 'He's putting on those green shoes, yes he is.'

■ Adapt the words to a sequence of things to be done to get ready for pre-school, for example 'We're waking up this morning, yes we are ... we're getting dressed this morning ... eating up our breakfast ... driving off to pre-school.'

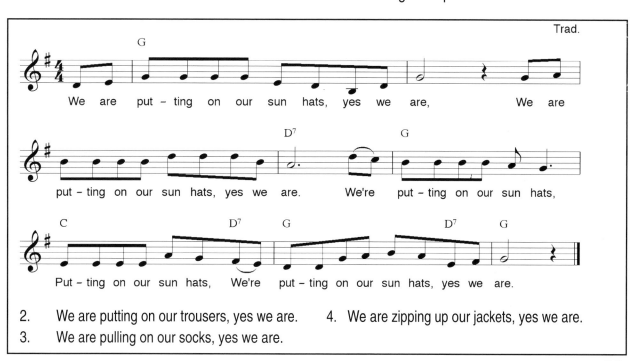

We are put-ting on our sun hats, yes we are, We are put-ting on our sun hats, yes we are. We're put-ting on our sun hats, Put-ting on our sun hats, We're put-ting on our sun hats, yes we are.

2. We are putting on our trousers, yes we are.
3. We are pulling on our socks, yes we are.

4. We are zipping up our jackets, yes we are.

Hand is walking

An action game

Age:	birth–2 years
Grouping:	individual, holding or nursing child on your lap
Resources:	none

How to play
- ◘ Hold the child safely in your arms.
- ◘ As you say the rhyme gently 'walk' your fingers up the child's arm, over the head and down the other arm.
- ◘ Repeat while child remains interested.

Variations
- ◘ You might like to 'walk' your fingers along the child's leg, over the tummy and down the other leg.
- ◘ Older/more experienced children often enjoy 'walking' their fingers over you as they imitate the game.

Rhyme

Hand is walking	*Walk your finger up one arm of the child.*
Hand is walking	
Walking up and over the hill	*Walk your fingers over the head of the child.*
Hand is jumping	*Jump your fingers up and down on child's arm.*
Hand is hopping	*Hop your fingers up and down on child's arm.*
And now hand is standing still.	*Hold your fingers still.*

Written by Veronicah Larkin and Louie Suthers
www.brilliantpublications.co.uk

Age:	2–5 years
Grouping:	small/medium group, large open space suitable for movement, indoor or outdoor environment
Resources:	a length of rope (2.5 metres, depending on the group size and available playing space); 4–8 hoops.

Hoops on a rope
A hoop game

How to play

- ❑ 2 adults hold the rope at each end at adult waist height (the exact height from the ground will be determined by the dimensions of the hoops and the age/size/experience of the children).
- ❑ The hoops are threaded along the rope at regular intervals.
- ❑ Invite the children to start at one end of the rope and walk/crawl/step through each hoop until they have reached the other end of the rope.
- ❑ Children can be encouraged to complete a circuit as many times as they like.

Variations

- ❑ Some younger/less experienced children prefer to have an adult near the hoop as they pass through it.
- ❑ Older/more experienced children can be encouraged to walk/crawl/step backwards through the hoops.

How do I feel?

A drama game

Age:	3–5 years
Grouping:	small/medium/large group, seated informally around an adult
Resources:	none

How to play

- Invite a child to stand in front of the group and 'make a face'. Examples might include happy, sad, angry, frightened, sleepy, scared, puzzled and brave.
- Encourage children to look carefully at 'the face' and decide what emotion the child is conveying.
- The game continues with a variety of children taking turns to 'make a face'.

Variations

- Children will sometimes accompany their facial expressions with a sound effect, such as a growling sound for 'angry', crying for 'sad', or a yawn for 'sleepy'. You might like to gently encourage older/more experienced children to use only their faces to convey their chosen emotions.
- You could make up a short story, such as 'It was Bobby's birthday, and when he opened his present it was a brand new computer game.' You can invite the children to show what sort of 'face' Bobby would have on his birthday.

Written by Veronicah Larkin and Louie Suthers
www.brilliantpublications.co.uk

Age:	2–5 years
Grouping:	individual/small/medium group large open space suitable for movement
Resources:	a variety of objects such as a feather, leaf, ball, balloon, cushion, scarf, small bean bag and confetti.

Imitating the fall
A falling game

How to play

- ❑ Encourage children to find a space in the room where they can move safely without bumping into others.
- ❑ In turn, hold an object above your head and allow it to fall to the ground. Encourage the children to observe the object closely as it falls, and then imitate the way the object travels through space and lands.
- ❑ Repeat the game using a variety of objects, while the children's interest is maintained.

Variations

- ❑ You can encourage the children to find common objects in the indoor and outdoor environments to use in this game.
- ❑ Older/more experienced children can be invited to examine the size/weight of an object and predict the way it might fall, and then test out their predictions by dropping the object and observing carefully.
- ❑ Other variations on falling, suitable for physically challenged children, may include children gently rolling/bouncing as they imitate a ball, or wriggling along the ground as they imitate a length of rope being shaken.

Indoor obstacle course

A movement game

Age:	2–5 years
Grouping:	individual/small/medium group
Resources:	a variety of items such as child-sized tables, chairs, cushions, hoops, ropes, large cardboard boxes.

How to play

- ◻ A collection of objects are placed in a large circle or along a straight line in the indoor environment. As it is an indoor obstacle course, it may be novel to choose objects not normally used in outdoor obstacle courses.

- ◻ Invite the children to make their way along the course, for example by climbing over the tables, crawling between the legs of the chairs, stepping through the hoops, jumping over the ropes and rolling along the cushions.

Variations

As in all obstacle courses, careful supervision is essential to ensure children's safety. You might like to encourage the children to choose the objects in the course, and to decide where they will be placed, and how they will be used. Encourage the children to undertake the course at their own pace to avoid a competitive atmosphere. You may need to make special provision for younger/ less experienced/less able children to enable their fullest involve- ment in the obstacle course.

Written by Veronicah Larkin and Louie Suthers
www.brilliantpublications.co.uk

Age:	2–5 years
Grouping:	individual/small/medium group, a long open space
Resources:	several large stackable blocks (or similar).

Jack be nimble

A movement game

How to play

- ◘ Familiarize the children with the rhyme Jack be nimble.
- ◘ Stack one or several blocks vertically to represent the candle. The height of the 'candle' will depend upon the age/ experience of the children.
- ◘ Invite a child to stand at a distance from the 'candle' and to run towards it, then to jump over it, as the remaining children say the rhyme.
- ◘ Offer interested children the chance to have a turn at jumping over the 'candle'.

Variations

- ◘ For older/more experienced children additional blocks may be added to provide a further challenge.
- ◘ Younger/less experienced children some-times prefer to hold your hand as they make the jump.
- ◘ You can substitute a female name, use names from a variety of cultures, or use the child's own name in place of 'Jack'.
- ◘ Another variation is to invite children to pretend they are an animal/insect that loves to jump like a frog, kangaroo, lamb, dolphin, antelope, grasshopper or even a flea.

Rhyme
Jack be nimble, Jack be quick,
Jack jump over the candlestick.

Jig jog
A knee-bouncing game

Age:	6 months–3 years
Grouping:	individual/small group
Resources:	none

How to play

- Sit child on your lap either facing towards or away from you.
- Sing song and sway the child from side to side or bounce the child on your lap. Bounce on the 'jig jog' part, sway for the rest (see below).

Variations

- Toddlers can play this game by sitting with you on the floor, alternately rocking from side to side and bouncing up and down.
- Older children can move around for this game, swaying in place and trotting around on the 'jig jogs'. Encourage them to sing (at least the 'jig jog' parts) as well as move around.
- The game can also be played with non-mobile children in pushchairs. Gently rock the push chair back and forwards in the 'jig jog' parts; push the pushchair around for the rest.

I want some-one to buy me a po-ny, jig jog, jig jog.
Not too fat and not too bo-ny,
jig-ga jog jig. For I want to go for a ride,
All a-round the coun-try side, With a jig jog, jig jog,
jig jog, jig jog, jig jog, jig-ga jog jig.

Written by Veronicah Larkin and Louie Suthers
www.brilliantpublications.co.uk

Josh goes high

A lap game

Age:	birth–2 years
Grouping:	individual, holding or nursing child
Resources:	none

How to play

- ◘ Hold the child safely in your arms.
- ◘ As you say the rhyme gently move the child up, down and from side to side.
- ◘ Repeat while child remains interested.

Variations

- ◘ Many older children enjoy the sensation of being lifted, lowered and swung from side to side with a little more vigour. It is important to undertake this with care, to ensure the child's safety and the well being of your back!

Rhyme

Josh goes high
Josh goes low
Josh goes side to side
Just so.

Substitute the child's name.

Written by Veronicah Larkin and Louie Suthers
www.brilliantpublications.co.uk

What will we play today?

Katie dances

A singing game
Tune: Old Macdonald had a farm

Age:	2–5 years
Grouping:	small/medium/large group, children standing in a circle
Resources:	none

How to play
◻ Invite one child to come into the middle of the circle.

◻ Children sing the song as the child in the middle devises an action for everyone to copy.

◻ On the last line of the song the child chooses a new child to come into the circle and the game continues in this manner.

Variations
◻ Substitute the child's own name for 'Katie'.

◻ You might like to choose 2 or more children to come into the circle together, and invent a shared action for everyone to copy.

◻ Where you are playing this game with an individual child you could change the last line of the song to 'I can do it too'.

Written by Veronicah Larkin and Louie Suthers
www.brilliantpublications.co.uk

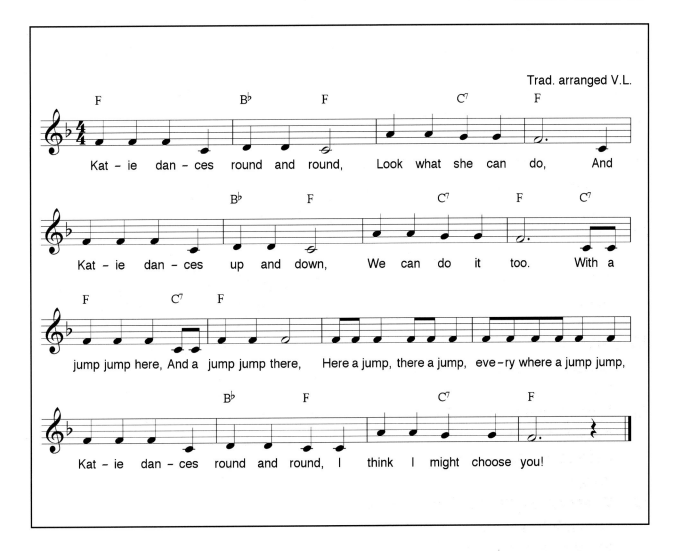

Katie dances round and round   *Child moves and dances freely in the middle of the circle.*

Look what she can do

And Katie dances up and down

We can do it too

With a ...   *Here child demonstrates an action*

And a ...   *(such as jump, nod, shake, bounce, twirl, bend).*

Here a ...

There a ...

Everywhere a ...

Katie dances round and round

I think I might choose you!   *Child points to the one she or he has chosen to have the next turn.*

Lap ball
A ball game

Age:	3–5 years
Grouping:	small/medium group, children seated on the floor in a line with legs stretched out in front of them (the children will have to sit very close to each other)
Resources:	a medium-sized plastic or rubber ball

How to play

- ◻ Place the ball on the lap of the first child, who transfers the ball to the next child's lap without using hands.
- ◻ This continues, with each child transferring the ball to the next child's lap, all without the use of hands.
- ◻ When the ball reaches the end of the line it can begin its journey back to the beginning of the line.

Variations

- ◻ A ball with a bell (or other sound maker) inside makes an interesting variation, and can assist the fuller participation of visually impaired children.
- ◻ For older/more experienced children the ball may be substituted for a small bean bag, a soft shoe (such as a slipper) or even a good-natured teddy bear or other cuddly toy.

Written by Veronicah Larkin and Louie Suthers
www.brilliantpublications.co.uk

Leg over leg

A lap game

How to play

◻ Sit child on your lap facing outwards. Hold the child's ankles and gently cross and uncross them as you say the rhyme.

◻ When you get to the 'Woooooooop' safely lift the child up as if you were going to tip him/her over your shoulder.

Variations

◻ Children will quickly learn the rhyme and sequence of movements, and laugh in anticipation of the 'jump'. You can surprise them by changing the speed of the rhyme and slowing or hurrying parts.

◻ Encourage the child to say the rhyme with you.

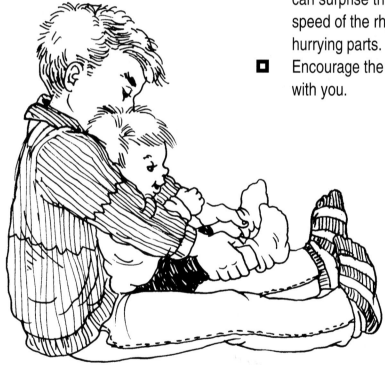

Rhyme

Leg over leg as the dog ran to Dover   *Cross and uncross child's legs.*

When he came to the fence
Wooooooooooooop! he jumped over.   *Lift child up.*

Little grey ponies

A movement game

Age:	3–5 years
Grouping:	small/medium/large group
Resources:	'barn' marked out on the floor

How to play

- ◘ All children start in the barn. They sing the song.
- ◘ On the line 'The little grey ponies jump over the fence,' the children jump out of the barn and gallop freely around the room.
- ◘ They continue to gallop around until the line 'The little grey ponies come back to the barn ... ' when they make their way back to the barn.
- ◘ On the last line 'The little grey ponies are having a rest ... ' the children lie down in the barn and pretend to sleep.
- ◘ Repeat as required.

Variations

- ◘ This game provides a playful context for children to practise their galloping.
- ◘ Vary the size of the barn; the larger the barn the more room the ponies have to sleep. In a smallish barn the children will have to huddle close to and on top of each other. Depending on the social development of the children, you may see this as a positive or negative aspect of the game.
- ◘ Older/more experienced children enjoy making their own barns using home corner equipment, wooden blocks or movable shelves.
- ◘ This game can be played as an outdoor drama game. The children can make a barn by draping a sheet across trees or outdoor equipment.
- ◘ Children with communication disabilities often enjoy making 'galloping music' for this game using woodblocks, sticks, coconut shells or castanets.

Written by Veronicah Larkin and Louie Suthers

www.brilliantpublications.co.uk

Little grey ponies

Trad.

The little grey ponies look over the fence,
The little grey ponies jump over the fence, And
over the fence to - day, way, And
gal - lop and gal - lop a - way, And
gal - lop and gal - lop a - way, And gal - lop and gal - lop a -
way. The lit - tle grey pon - ies come back to the barn,
back to the barn to stay. The lit - tle grey pon - ies are
hav - ing a rest, hav - ing a rest from their play.

Little red wagon

A movement game

How to play

- ◻ Sing the song and bounce up and down. For the second verse sway from side to side as you sing about the aeroplane. Repeat the first verse. Continue to alternate the contrasting verses as appropriate.

Variations

- ◻ Play the game with younger babies as a knee-bouncing game, alternately bouncing and swaying the child on your knee.
- ◻ Use other forms of transport, such as 'Hurrying along in my little black steam train' or 'Sailing along in my little white sailing boat' and devise matching actions.
- ◻ Play with the children bouncing on a mini-trampoline.

Age:	1–3 years
Grouping:	individual/small/medium group
Resources:	none

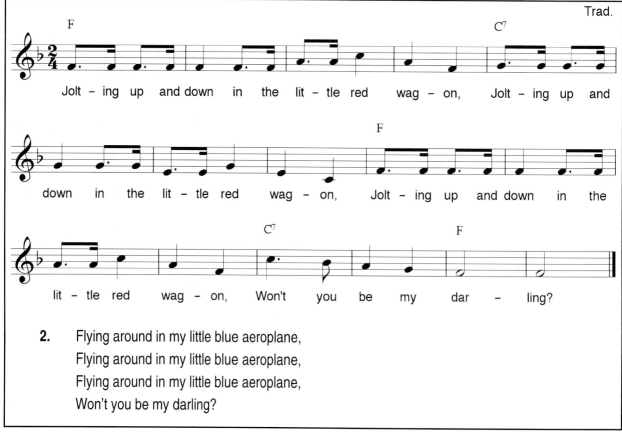

Jolt – ing up and down in the lit – tle red wag – on, Jolt – ing up and down in the lit – tle red wag – on, Jolt – ing up and down in the lit – tle red wag – on, Won't you be my dar – ling?

2. Flying around in my little blue aeroplane,
   Flying around in my little blue aeroplane,
   Flying around in my little blue aeroplane,
   Won't you be my darling?

Written by Veronicah Larkin and Louie Suthers

www.brilliantpublications.co.uk

Age:	3–5 years
Grouping:	small/medium/large group, children gathered informally around an adult
Resources:	a 'looky lucky' looking frame (see details below)

Looky lucky detective

A work-it-out game

How to play

- Invite a child to take the looky lucky looking frame and move freely around the space.
- Encourage the child to observe the environment closely, just like a detective, by looking through the looky lucky. The child decides upon an item seen through the looky lucky and joins the other children again.
- The group says the rhyme and then begins the task of finding out what the detective saw through the looky lucky by asking questions, such as 'What colour is it?'
- The game continues until the children have identified the item.

Variations

- This is not a guessing game as the children are encouraged to think of questions that will assist them to work out the correct answer.
- This game can be played in an indoor or outdoor environment.
- For older/more experienced children the game can be adapted for use on public transport, such as during an outing. The detective child can look through the looky lucky at an item of interest, observed through the window, and the remaining children can determine what that item is.

How to make a looky lucky

An old hand held mirror (with the mirror part missing) or an old magnifying glass (with the glass missing) makes an ideal frame for the child to look through. Alternatively you could make a looking frame by using sturdy cardboard and decorating it with paint, glitter, collage or other scrap materials.

Rhyme

Looky lucky licky law
I wonder what Maria saw.
Substitute childs name.

Make a cake

An action game

Age: 12 months–3 years
Grouping: individual/small group
Resources: optional sand or play dough

How to play

☐ Say the rhyme below, holding the baby's hands gently, and do the actions. Repeat as required.

Variations

☐ Older children can do the actions themselves.

☐ Use sand or play dough.

☐ Change what is being made to a pizza, a pie or whatever else is familiar to the children.

☐ Use the traditional nursery rhyme Pat-a-cake, pat-a-cake in a similar way.

Rhyme

Make a cake, cake, cake	*Pat baby's hands together on each 'cake'*
Make it flat, flat, flat	*Pat baby's hands onto his/her knees.*
Make a cake, cake, cake	*Pat baby's hands together.*
Just like that!	*Both hands out, palms up.*
	Lift both arms above head.

Age:	4–5 years
Grouping:	small group, seated cross-legged in a close circle
Resources:	a shoe (or small bean bag) for each player

Mal mal

A passing game

How to play

- Learn the song very well. Tap floor, knees and other body parts in slow steady beat. This is indicated by * in the music. It is essential that the children know the song very well before the passing game is attempted.
- Sing song and tap shoes to beat. Every one holds shoes in right hand and puts left hand behind back or sits on it. Always tap the shoe in front of self then to right.
- When everyone can sing and tap shoe to the beat, try the passing game. Each time you tap a shoe to the right, leave it on the floor (in front of your neighbour). Then there should be another shoe in front of you. In this way all the shoes are passed around the circle. Repeat the song as many times as it takes for everyone to get their own shoe back, or until there is a large pile of shoes in front of one player.

Variations

- If the children can play this game they are doing very well and you probably won't feel any need to challenge their co-ordination and co-operation.

Trad. New Guinea

Mal, mal, mal, Kam - em - e go, Kam - em - e

go, Kal - um - bus, Kal - um - bus.

Manual road

A passing game

Age:	4–5 years
Grouping:	small group, seated cross-legged in a close circle
Resources:	a shoe (or small bean bag) for each player

How to play

- ◻ Learn the song Manual Road. As part of learning the song children should tap the beats marked * very rhythmically on their knees or other body parts.

- ◻ When the song is known well, use shoes or whatever is to be passed in the pattern – tap the floor in front of you, then tap the floor to your right. It is essential that everyone taps in the same pattern and direction or passing the shoes will not work. Practise the tapping pattern until the group can do it confidently.

- ◻ Try passing by letting go of the shoe when it is placed to the right. There should be a new shoe then waiting in front of each player. Continue to pass until the shoes come around the circle to their owners, or the passing becomes dysfunctional. You'll probably make several attempts before it works. Don't be disheartened; it's great when it finally works.

Variations

- ◻ Add new verses by continuing the counting sequence. Try other passing games such as Mal mal or Obwisana.

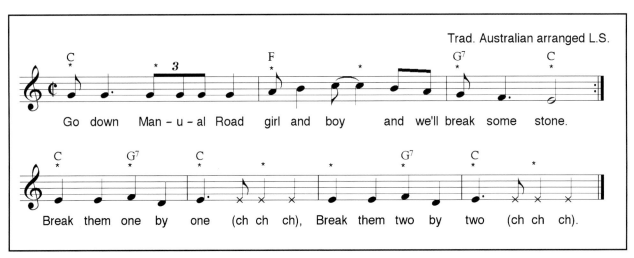

Trad. Australian arranged L.S.

Go down Man – u – al Road girl and boy and we'll break some stone.

Break them one by one (ch ch ch), Break them two by two (ch ch ch).

Written by Veronicah Larkin and Louie Suthers

www.brilliantpublications.co.uk

Age:	2–5 years
Grouping:	individual/small group
Resources:	up to 5 pairs of shakers – all the shakers should be made from identical opaque plastic bottles, containers of differing size or shape will make different sounds (refer to notes regarding further preparation of shakers).

Match the shakers
A listening game

How to play

- ▪ Start with 4 shakers (2 pairs). Children listen to each shaker and match the pairs.
- ▪ Add more pairs of shakers as the children gain experience and confidence.

Variations

- ▪ The children can arrange the pairs of shakers from softest to loudest.
- ▪ Older children may enjoy making and decorating their own shaker sets to try on you and their friends.
- ▪ Children with visual disabilities often have acute listening skills. You'll find they are excellent at most listening games. Older children who are not worried by being blind-folded may enjoy the challenge of playing this game with their eyes covered.
- ▪ These shakers can be used for other games such as Sound moves, Follow the sound or Spot the difference.

Note

To prepare shakers, fill pairs of bottles with the same quantity of various foodstuffs such as flour, rice, cereal, lentils or pasta; then seal them securely. Medical practitioners recommend that only foodstuffs be used as they will cause the least concern in case of accidental swallowing or inhalation. For your reference, it is useful to mark the shakers as pairs in some discreet way.

Mother and Father and Uncle John

A knee-bouncing game

How to play

- Say the rhyme and bounce the child rhythmically on your knee as you do so.

Variations

- Physically timid children will need the reassurance of eye contact, so sit them on your knee facing you and hold them securely under the arms. Other children will enjoy very vigorous bouncing and pretend falling off. They will prefer to face away from you into the room. Generally, older children enjoy more boisterous play.

Age:	5 months–2 years
Grouping:	individual
Resources:	none

Rhyme

Mother and Father and Uncle John	*Bounce child on knee.*
Went to town upon a ram	
Mother fell off	*Lean child far over to the left.*
Father fell off	*Lean child far over to the right.*
But Uncle John went on and on	*Bounce again and get faster*
and on and on and on …*	*and faster.*

Written by Veronicah Larkin and Louie Suthers
www.brilliantpublications.co.uk

Age:	2–5 years
Grouping:	small/medium group, informally gathered around an adult
Resources:	dressing-up clothes; home corner furniture; dramatic play props as desired.

A drama game

Tune: Miss Polly had a dolly

How to play

- Acquaint the children with the song.
- Invite one child to play the role of Mr Eddy, one to play the teddy and one to play the doctor.
- Assist the children to choose dressing-up clothes and props as they wish. Of course, it is not necessary to prepare an elaborate performance, and the game can be played without any such additions.
- Mr Eddy, the teddy and the doctor enact the song as the remaining children sing.
- The game continues with interested children taking the roles.

Variations

- Older/more experienced children often enjoy the words and/or stories of familiar songs and rhymes. Perhaps you could give some thought to inventing new characters and situations using the children's favourite songs and rhymes.
- Additionally, you could examine the material you currently share with the children. Can you devise words that may be more gender-inclusive and culture-inclusive?

1. The doctor came with her bag and her hat, And she knocked on the door with a rat-a-tat-tat.

2. She looked at the teddy and she shook her head. She said 'Mr Eddy put him straight to bed. I'll write on a paper for a pill, pill, pill. I'll be back in the morning, yes I will, will, will!'

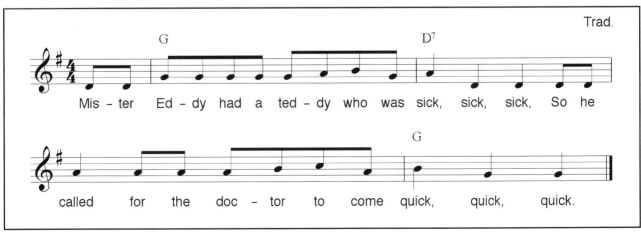

Mis-ter Ed – dy had a ted – dy who was sick, sick, sick, So he called for the doc – tor to come quick, quick, quick.

Musical hoops

A hoop game

<table>
<tr><td>Age:</td><td>2–5 years</td></tr>
<tr><td>Grouping:</td><td>small/medium group</td></tr>
<tr><td>Resources:</td><td>a set of 4–6 hoops (the exact number will depend upon the size of the group and the available playing space), recorded music</td></tr>
</table>

How to play

- Place the hoops randomly on the floor. There should be sufficient space between each hoop so that children can move comfortably and safely between them.
- As the music plays encourage the children to move/dance around the room and in between the hoops.
- When the music stops invite the children to find a hoop and stand in it.
- Repeat the game while the children maintain interest.

Variations

- This is not a competitive game as more than one child can stand in the same hoop and no child needs to be eliminated.
- For older/more experienced children you might like to direct them towards a particular hoop, for example 'When the music stops try and find a yellow hoop.'
- As you repeat the game you can gradually take some hoops away, which will require the children to 'squash' into the remaining hoops. Ensure that this can be done in safety.
- You could vary the positions of the hoops in the room as the game progresses.
- Another variation is to hold up the hoops (parallel to the floor at adult waist height) and invite the children to bob under, and stand up inside, the hoop when the music stops.
- Alternatives to hoops might include musical cushions, where a number of children can sit on the same cushion together, or musical boxes, where a number of children can crawl into, or stand up, in a cardboard box together.
- For older/more experienced children you could invite them to find a hoop when the music changes (rather than simply when the music stops).

Written by Veronicah Larkin and Louie Suthers
www.brilliantpublications.co.uk

Age:	4–5 years
Grouping:	small/medium/large group, seated in a circle
Resources:	a small egg (plastic or wooden)

My little hen (Mi Gallinita)

A listening game
How to play

◻ One child is chosen to be the hen. This child walks around the circle and hides the egg by giving it to another child. Another child is chosen to be listener, and sits in the middle of the circle with eyes covered.

◻ Everyone sings the song as the hen hides her egg. On the last line, only the child with the egg sings. The listener then tries to identify who has the egg. The child who had the egg becomes the hen and a new listener is chosen. Repeat as many times as you wish.

◻ Play the game in both English and Spanish.

Note

Most children are quite unselfconscious about singing on their own; and they only have to sing one note. However if this proves difficult, the game works just as well with chicken noises rather than a sung last line.

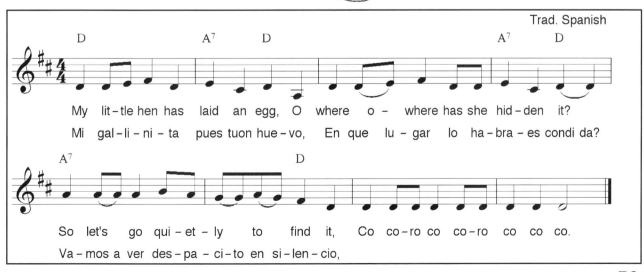

Trad. Spanish

My lit-tle hen has laid an egg, O where o-where has she hid-den it?
Mi gal-li-ni-ta pues tuon hue-vo, En que lu-gar lo ha-bra-es condi da?

So let's go qui-et-ly to find it, Co co-ro co co-ro co co co.
Va-mos a ver des-pa-ci-to en si-len-cio,

Newspaper game

A following game

Age:	2–5 years
Grouping:	small/medium group, sitting around an adult or in a circle
Resources:	a sheet of newspaper for each player

How to play

- Everyone sings the song. At the end of the song the leader makes a sound with her newspaper and everyone copies it.
- Newspaper sounds might include rustling, waving, scrunching, tearing, rubbing or flicking.
- Repeat the game as many times as required or until the newspaper disintegrates. The last action to copy should be putting it in a box or recycling bin.

Variations

- Encourage the children to take turns in being the leader and devising new sounds. You may find that children who are reluctant to move or express themselves verbally in a large group don't mind demonstrating a new sound or idea with their newspaper.
- The game can also be used for follow-the-leader actions or body sounds.

Trad. American

Do what I'm do-ing, Fol-low, fol-low me. Do what I'm do-ing, Fol-low, fol-low me.

Written by Veronicah Larkin and Louie Suthers

www.brilliantpublications.co.uk

Age:	4–5 years
Grouping:	small/medium group, seated cross-legged in a close circle
Resources:	a bean bag or shoe for each player – in Africa, the game is traditionally played with stones (as these are considered too dangerous for young children to use, substitute with any objects that are easy to pick up and will not roll away).

Obwisana

A passing game

How to play

- Learn the song very well. Tap floor, knees and other body parts in slow steady beat. This is indicated by * in the music. It is important that everyone knows the song well before you play the passing game

- Sing song and tap bean bags/shoes to beat. Everyone holds bean bag/shoe in right-hand and puts left hand behind back or sits on it. Always tap the bean bag/shoe in front of yourself then to right. It is often difficult for the children opposite you in the circle to get their movements to match the group's because they have to reverse what they see you doing.

- When everyone can sing and tap to the beat, try the passing game. Each time you tap a bean bag/shoe to the right, leave it on the floor (in front of your neighbour). Then there should be another waiting in front of you. In this way all the bean bags/shoes are passed around the circle. Repeat song as many times as required.

Variations

- Try passing to the left with left hands.

Note

Obwisana means 'A stone fell on my hand.'

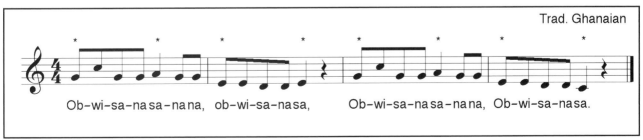

Written by Veronicah Larkin and Louie Suthers
www.brilliantpublications.co.uk

What will we play today?

One in the middle

A movement game

Age:	2–5 years
Grouping:	small/medium/large group, standing in circle
Resources:	none

How to play

- One child in the centre of the circle jumps up and down. The others clap and sing the song.
- The child in the middle chooses a friend, and the words change to 'Two in the middle ... '
- Each child in the middle chooses a friend, and the words change to 'Four in the middle ... '
- Everyone takes a small step into the circle, and the words change to 'All in the middle ... jump everyone'.

Variations

- Change the words to a different sequence depending on the numbers of children in the middle. For example instead of doubling, have 1, 2, 3, 4, 5 ... in the middle; the most recent child chooses a friend at the end of each verse.
- Double four and eight as well as one and two, if this is appropriate for the group.
- Change the actions that the rest of the group does from clapping to patting knees or tapping other body parts.

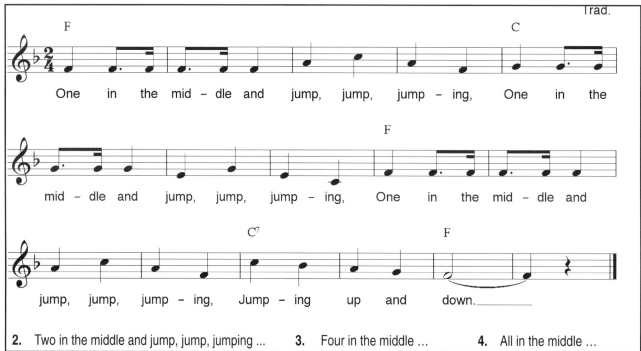

2. Two in the middle and jump, jump, jumping ...   3. Four in the middle ...   4. All in the middle ...

Written by Veronicah Larkin and Louie Suthers

www.brilliantpublications.co.uk

One two

Age:	2½–5 years
Grouping:	small/medium/large group, seated in a circle
Resources:	a pair of sticks for each player

A stick game

How to play

- Say the rhyme and do actions as indicated.
- Repeat as many times as you wish.

Variations

- Count to 20 and invent stick actions to match.
- Use other rhymes and chants and add stick actions.
- Encourage children who can speak another language to help the others learn to count to ten in their language. Substitute these for 'one, two' 'three, four'... in the counting sequence of the game.

Rhyme

● ● ◉ ◉ ◉
One, two, tap your shoe
● ● ◆ ◆ ◆
Three, four, bang the floor
● ● ❖ ❖ ❖
Five, six, hammer your sticks

● ● ■
Seven, eight, lay them straight
● ● ✡
Nine, ten, do it all again.

● = tap sticks

◉ = tap shoe three times

◆ = bang the floor three times

❖ = hammer; hold one stick like a big nail and hammer it three times

■ = place sticks on floor

✡ = roll sticks around

Over the stones

A knee-bouncing game

Age:	6 months–3 years
Grouping:	individual/small group, babies – knee-bouncing toddlers – informally gathered around an adult
Resources:	none

How to play

◘ Adult sings song and bounces baby.

◘ Toddlers can bounce themselves either sitting on the floor/ground or standing.

Variations

◘ Bounce over other things besides stones, for example hills, bridges, tracks, speed bumps.

◘ This song is very effective as a travelling song on excursions; the children enjoy lots of verses!

◘ 'Over the stones … ' could be changed to 'in outer space … ' for older children who love travelling by rocket. Other changes might include 'over the waves' for travelling by boat or 'over the tracks' for train travel.

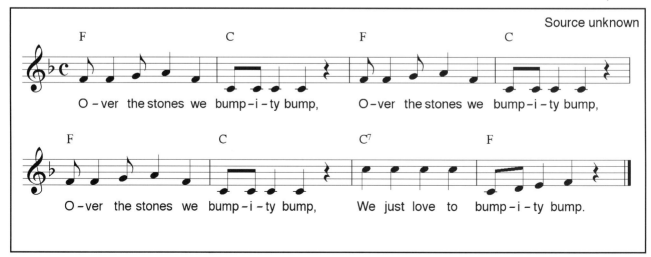

Source unknown

O – ver the stones we bump – i – ty bump,   O – ver the stones we bump – i – ty bump,

O – ver the stones we bump – i – ty bump,   We just love to bump – i – ty bump.

Written by Veronicah Larkin and Louie Suthers
www.brilliantpublications.co.uk

Age:	2–5 years
Grouping:	small/medium group, children standing/seated in a line
Resources:	shaker (or similar sound maker)

Pass the shaker

A passing game

How to play

- ◘ Invite one child to stand at a distance from the line, with eyes closed, being the 'listener'.
- ◘ Encourage each child to shake the sound maker, and then pass it on to the next child along the line.
- ◘ At some point along the line indicate to a child to shake the sound maker and then hold it behind her/his back.
- ◘ Invite the 'listener' child to open her/his eyes and work out where the sound has stopped along the line, and who is holding the sound maker.
- ◘ Repeat the game, offering a variety of children the opportunity to be the 'listener'.

Variations

- ◘ You can encourage older/more experienced children to shake the sound maker behind their backs and then pass it along, behind them, to the next child in the line.
- ◘ You might like to sing a passing song (or any favourite tune) as you pass the shaker.

Peek-a-boo

A hiding game

Age:	8 months–2 years
Grouping:	individual
Resources:	none

How to play

- ❑ Sing the song while you cover and uncover your eyes with your hands. Some children will just watch while others will imitate your actions. With young babies you can also use your hands to cover and uncover their eyes.

Variations

- ❑ Use a sheet, blanket, cushion, large soft toy or other object to hold up and lower as appropriate or look around the sides.
- ❑ Play peek-a-boo with a favourite toy that can be hidden (or partially hidden) around the room. Substitute the toy's name into the words of the song, for example 'Peek-a-boo where is Ted? Where is Ted hiding now?' Keep singing the song until the toy is discovered.
- ❑ With an older/more experienced child, take turns at hiding and covering your eyes.

Written by Veronicah Larkin and Louie Suthers
www.brilliantpublications.co.uk

People skittles

A falling game

Age:	3–5 years
Grouping:	small/medium group, large open space suitable for movement
Resources:	a soft plastic or rubber ball

How to play

- Invite children to stand together in a triangle shape. Depending on the group size this might mean four children in the back row, three children in the middle row and two children in the front row. All children should stand quite close together and face in the same direction.
- Invite a child to stand a distance away and roll the ball along the ground towards the 'skittles'.
- The children are encouraged to fall over if they feel the ball touching their legs, or if they are touched by a nearby falling child.

Notes

Children often enjoy deliberately falling over, however, you should remind children to fall gently and carefully so that they do not harm themselves or other children.

This game can be played in an indoor or outdoor environment, wherever there is a soft fall area. This game should not be played on concrete or similar surfaces.

Person obstacle course

A movement game

Age:	2–5 years
Grouping:	small/medium group, large open space suitable for movement
Resources:	none

How to play

- ❑ This game will require a number of willing adults or older children.
- ❑ The game follows the same principle as a conventional obstacle course; however, instead of equipment the children are invited to scramble under, over and through people.
- ❑ Place the adults in the formation of your choice (it might be circular, in a long line or at random). Each adult adopts a frozen position and children can negotiate the course, with your help.
- ❑ Some positions might include:
  – standing with legs apart for children to crawl through;
  – bending over and touching the floor with hands so children can tunnel throug;
  – kneeling down with hands stretched out in front to form a ring for children to step in and out of;
  – lying flat on the floor with arms together and legs together for children to step over;
  – crouching with knees and hands touching the floor (a table shape) for children to wriggle under.
- ❑ Encourage children to complete the circuit at their own pace.

Variations

- ❑ Invite the children to assist you in devising the course, including directing the adults in how and where to stand.
- ❑ This game may be played in an indoor environment or on a soft fall surface in an outdoor environment.
- ❑ As in all obstacle courses, careful supervision is essential to ensure children's safety.

Written by Veronicah Larkin and Louie Suthers
www.brilliantpublications.co.uk

Age:	6 months–3 years
Grouping:	individual
Resources:	none

Pizza, sausage
A tickling game

How to play

◻ Baby lies on his/her back on the floor. Hold baby's wrists and gently clap his/her hands together gently as you say the rhyme. At the end tickle the baby all over.

Variations

◻ Touch three places on baby's body (eg hair, chest, feet) as you say the name of the three foods then tickle.

◻ An older child, sitting or standing close, can clap both hands together with you before you tickle his/her tummy; or you can hold one of the child's hands and clap your other hand on that.

Rhyme

Pizza, sausage, pumpernickel	*Clap.*
This little tummy will have a tickle.	*Clap then tickle tummy on 'tickle'.*

Polly whoops!

A tickling game

How to play

- Hold child's hand and say the rhyme. As you say it, touch each finger tip in turn, starting with the little finger. The 'Whoops' coincides with the swoop between the first finger and the thumb. Run your finger up or down that shape as you say 'Whoops'.
- Repeat several times changing the speed or the volume of the rhyme.

Variations

- Use the child's name instead of 'Polly'.
- Play it as a knee-bouncing game with the child facing you. Bounce on 'Polly' and tip to the side on 'whoops'.
- Older toddlers enjoy playing this as a jumping game; jumping on 'Polly' and falling down and getting up on 'Whoops'.

Age:	6 months–2 years
Grouping:	individual, holding or nursing child
Resources:	none

Rhyme

Polly, Polly, Polly
Polly, Whoops!
Polly, Whoops!
Polly, Polly, Polly, Polly.

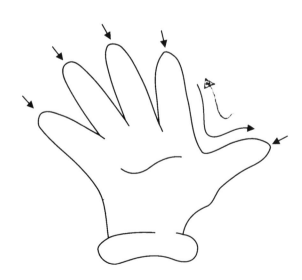

Written by Veronicah Larkin and Louie Suthers
www.brilliantpublications.co.uk

Age:	4–5 years
Grouping:	small/large group, line headed by an adult, other adults strategically placed through the line, large, open space
Resources:	1 shaker

Rattlesnake

A line game

How to play

◻ Everybody holds hands to form a line. The line becomes the snake. The person at the tail end of the line holds the shaker and rattles it at any time.

◻ Sing the song and walk around.

◻ The leader traces out patterns and the line snakes around behind. For example:

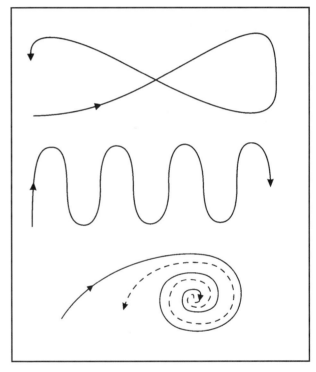

Variations

◻ Play the game outside and snake around the outdoor area.

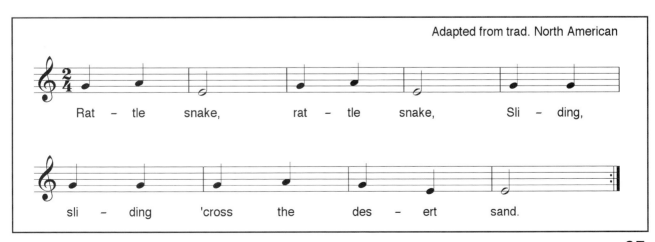

Adapted from trad. North American

Rat – tle snake, rat – tle snake, Sli – ding,

sli – ding 'cross the des – ert sand.

Ride baby ride

A knee-bouncing game

Age:	6 months–3 years
Grouping:	individual
Resources:	none

How to play

◘ Sit with the child on the floor. Position the child to face you on your lap or out-stretched legs.

◘ Sing the song as you bounce the child up and down. When you get to the last 'Whooa', gently tip the child over backwards.

◘ Repeat as many times as the child wants or as many times as your knees can stand.

Variations

◘ Substitute the child's name for 'baby' in the words of the song.

◘ Change the action to sway, rock, twirl or any other actions you can do holding the child.

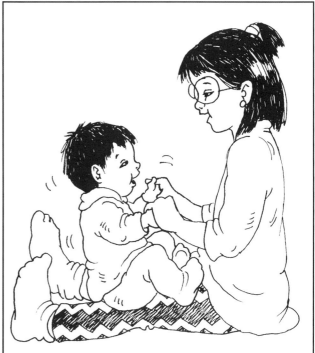

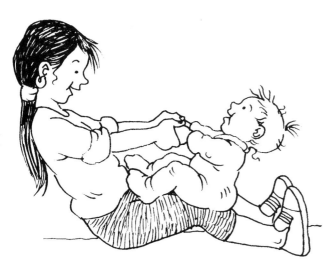

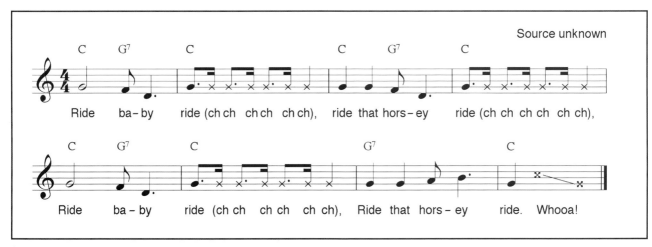

Source unknown

Ride ba–by ride (ch ch ch ch ch ch), ride that hors–ey ride (ch ch ch ch ch ch),

Ride ba–by ride (ch ch ch ch ch ch), Ride that hors–ey ride. Whooa!

Written by Veronicah Larkin and Louie Suthers

www.brilliantpublications.co.uk

Age:	18 months–5 years
Grouping:	individual/small/medium/large group; younger children can play this game gathered around an adult; older/more experienced children form a standing circle
Resources:	none

Ring a-ring a-rosy (giro giro tondo)

A falling game

How to play

◻ Sing the song as you jump up and down or clap and fall down at the end.

◻ Say the chant as you hit the floor/ground and jump at the end ready to repeat the game.

Variations

◻ Giro giro tondo is an Italian version of the same game. The tune is also very similar. Use the games interchangeably, alternating English and Italian.

◻ Play it as a circle game. Either stand in place and jump or clap, or walk around the circle singing.

◻ Play it as a knee-bouncing game with a baby. Have the baby facing you. On 'down' lower the baby backwards and on 'up' hold the baby in the air.

Spoken:
Cows are in the meadow eating buttercups,
Thunder and lightning we all jump up.

Roll that big ball

A ball game

Age:	18 months–4 years
Grouping:	small group, seated on the floor around the edge of a mat or in a circle
Resources:	1 large ball

How to play

- Roll the ball to one child, who rolls it back to you. Repeat with next child.
- Sing the song as the ball is rolled. Encourage children to sing and roll the ball.
- When the children know the song well, they can roll the ball to anyone in the group rather than back to you.

Variations

- Change the weather in the last line according to the day; 'sunny' can become 'rainy', 'windy', 'freezing' ...
- Substitute bouncing or throwing.
- With older/more experienced children, play the game in a line formation.
- Leader rolls the ball to each child in the line. Last child keeps the ball and becomes the leader; previous leader goes to the head of the line. Continue game until all children have had a turn as leader.

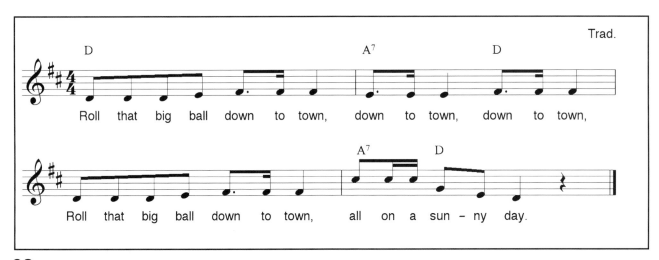

Trad.

Roll that big ball down to town, down to town, down to town,

Roll that big ball down to town, all on a sun – ny day.

Written by Veronicah Larkin and Louie Suthers

www.brilliantpublications.co.uk

Roll the ball

A ball game

Age:	6 months–3 years
Grouping:	individual/small group, seated on the floor with sufficient space between players to roll the ball; children find it easiest to sit with legs splayed
Resources:	1 large ball

How to play

- Roll the ball to the child and encourage the child to push it back to you.
- Sing the song as you roll the ball. Most younger children will probably focus on the physical activity only.
- Change the words to include the name of the child who will catch and roll the ball.

Variations

- Substitute 'bounce' or 'throw' the ball for children who can manage these skills.

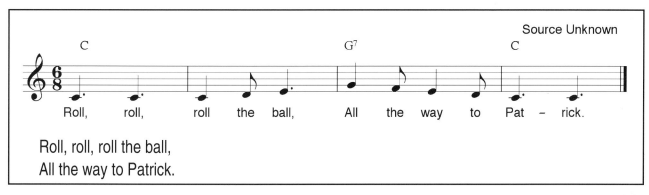

Source Unknown

Roll, roll, roll the ball, All the way to Pat-rick.

Roll, roll, roll the ball,
All the way to Patrick.

Written by Veronicah Larkin and Louie Suthers
www.brilliantpublications.co.uk

Round Australia

A movement game

Age:	4–5 years
Grouping:	small/medium/large group, circle or gathered informally around adult
Resources:	none

How to play

- The song is an echo song, so the children can play the game immediately by echoing (copying) each line after you.
- At first, just do the actions indicated throughout each verse.
- When the children are ready, change the game so that the actions accumulate. When playing the cumulative version, introduce every new action at the end of each verse.

Variations

- Children often enjoy an invented story about 'my aunt who used to travel all around Australia and brought back interesting things for me' as an introduction to the game.
- Change the game to include the names of other countries.

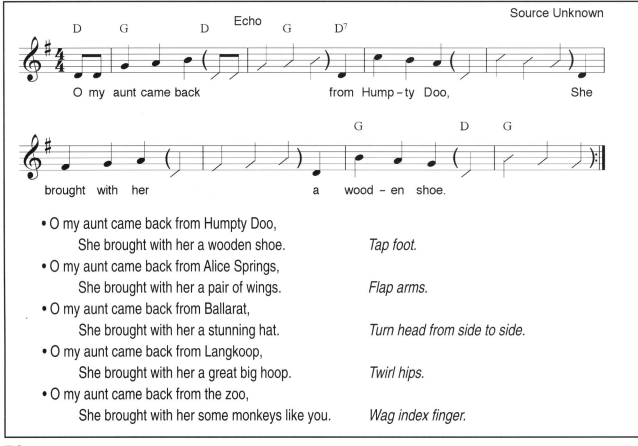

Source Unknown

O my aunt came back from Hump-ty Doo, She brought with her a wood-en shoe.

- O my aunt came back from Humpty Doo,
   She brought with her a wooden shoe.   *Tap foot.*
- O my aunt came back from Alice Springs,
   She brought with her a pair of wings.   *Flap arms.*
- O my aunt came back from Ballarat,
   She brought with her a stunning hat.   *Turn head from side to side.*
- O my aunt came back from Langkoop,
   She brought with her a great big hoop.   *Twirl hips.*
- O my aunt came back from the zoo,
   She brought with her some monkeys like you.   *Wag index finger.*

Written by Veronicah Larkin and Louie Suthers

www.brilliantpublications.co.uk

Sandy girl

A singing game

<table>
<tr><td>Age:</td><td>2–5 years</td></tr>
<tr><td>Grouping:</td><td>small/medium/large group, seated in a circle</td></tr>
<tr><td>Resources:</td><td>none</td></tr>
</table>

How to play

- Everyone sits in a circle; Sandy girl sits in the middle. Everyone sings the song, keeping the beat on their knees, shoulders or other body parts. This can change each time.

- Sandy girl acts out the appropriate parts of the song: 'crying', 'stand up', 'wipe your tears away', 'choose the one'…

- On the chorus Sandy girl and her friend hold hands and dance. Everyone else sings and claps. At the end of the chorus, the chosen child becomes the new Sandy girl/boy.

Source Unknown

See the lit – tle Sand – y girl/boy sit – ting on a stone,___ S/he's cry – ing s/he's cry – ing be – cause s/he's all a – lone.___ Stand up Sand – y girl/boy, wipe your tears a – way,___ Choose the one you like the best and take them out to play.___

Sandy girl/boy chooses friend

Chorus

Tra la la la la la la la...

Written by Veronicah Larkin and Louie Suthers
www.brilliantpublications.co.uk

What will we play today?

Shopping spree

A drama game

How to play

- A group of children take the roles of the shopkeepers and another group take the roles of the shoppers.
- The shopkeepers stand at intervals throughout the room and set up their shops, using dramatic play props.
- The shoppers move amongst the shopkeepers and have a shopping spree!
- Some suggestions for shops might include a hairdressing salon, veterinary surgery, dental clinic, medical centre, travel agent, supermarket, toy shop, shoe shop, police and ambulance stations.
- Encourage children to suggest their own ideas for stories related to shopping.

Variations

- This game can also be played with great success in an outdoor environment, with an emphasis on creative dramatic play related to outdoor shopping, such as markets, fêtes or fairs.

Age:	3–5 years
Grouping:	medium/large group, large open space in an indoor or outdoor environment
Resources:	dramatic play props, such as dressing-up clothes, hats, scarves, bags, shoes, empty food packages, pretend money

Written by Veronicah Larkin and Louie Suthers
www.brilliantpublications.co.uk

Snaky rope

A rope game

Age:	2–5 years
Grouping:	individual/small group, an open space suitable for movement
Resources:	a length of rope approximately 2–4 metres, depending on the group size and the available playing space

How to play

- Hold one end of the rope and allow the other end to trail along the ground.
- Invite children to follow the 'snake' as it slithers and slides around the space.
- The pace and amount of movement will depend upon the age/experience of the children.
- Continue to play while children remain interested.

Variations

- For older/more experienced children, a second adult with a second rope can be added to the game. The children can be encouraged to observe closely and to follow only the rope which is in motion. The two adults can alternate randomly between moving their rope and remaining motionless.
- To assist visually impaired children's participation in this game, you could tie a number of small bells at intervals along the rope so that the children can 'hear' where the rope is moving.

Written by Veronicah Larkin and Louie Suthers
www.brilliantpublications.co.uk

Sound moves

A listening game

How to play

- Choose 2 musical instruments/sound makers and invite children to demonstrate the sound produced by each.
- Once children are acquainted with the sounds, demonstrate an action to match each sound, such as 'when the triangle sounds we can walk on our toes with our hands high above us, and when the drum sounds we can crouch down low and stamp our feet.'
- Play each instrument in turn and encourage the children to listen carefully, and to demonstrate the appropriate action to match the sound as they move around the room.
- Continue to play while children's interest is maintained.

Variations

- For younger/less experienced children the 2 instruments should produce markedly different sounds. For older/more experienced children this is less crucial.
- An additional challenge, for older/more experienced children, is to have 2 adults playing 2 instruments each. You can then provide 4 actions to match the 4 sounds.
- Invite children to suggest actions.
- This game can be played in an indoor or outdoor environment.

Age:	2–5 years
Grouping:	small/medium/large group, large open space suitable for movement
Resources:	2 musical instruments/sound makers

Written by Veronicah Larkin and Louie Suthers
www.brilliantpublications.co.uk

Age:	2–5 years
Grouping:	individual/small/medium group, children gathered informally around adult
Resources:	2 pillow cases, 2 musical instruments/sound makers

Spot the difference

A listening game

How to play

- ◻ Play each instrument in turn and encourage children to listen carefully to both sounds.
- ◻ Invite children to close their eyes, while you place one instrument in one pillow case and one instrument in the other.
- ◻ Ask a child to shake a pillow case and identify the instrument by listening to the sound produced.

Variations

- ◻ For younger/less experienced children you could leave identical instruments in view, to assist in identification without the necessity for naming the instrument.
- ◻ Older/more experienced children can be additionally challenged by having 4 different instruments in 4 pillow cases to identify.
- ◻ Alternatives to pillow cases might be sealed boxes, non-see-through tupperware containers or draw-string bags.

Squeeze the ball and pass it on

A ball game
Tune: London Bridge

Age:	18 months–4 years
Grouping:	small group, in a circle formation
Resources:	5 or 6 small squeeze balls; foam or squashy rubber balls or bean bags can be used

How to play

◻ Squeeze the ball and pass it to the person on your right. With very young children it is best to have one ball per child. Initially, you may have to help them pass the ball as they often like to hold it.

◻ Sing the song as the balls are squeezed and passed. Most young children will probably focus on the physical activity only.

◻ As the children become more skilful, you can increase the size of the group or reduce the number of balls used.

◻ This game is good for children with visual disabilities. Select a variety of objects with differing tactile sensations. Change the words to 'Feel the … and pass it on.' Insert the name of each object and repeat the verse as many times as required.

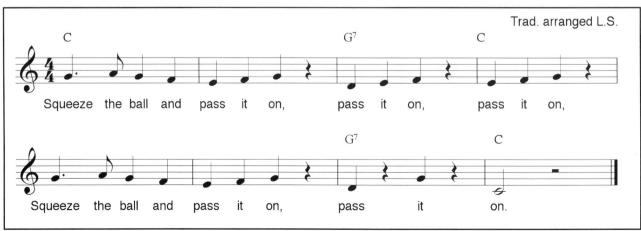

Trad. arranged L.S.

Squeeze the ball and pass it on, pass it on, pass it on,

Squeeze the ball and pass it on, pass it on.

Written by Veronicah Larkin and Louie Suthers

www.brilliantpublications.co.uk

Stop and go

A drama game

Age:	2 –5 years
Grouping:	small/medium group, large open space suitable for movement
Resources:	2 paper/plastic plates, 1 red and 1 green for the traffic lights

How to play

- Invite a child to take on the role of the police officer. This child stands in the middle of the room or safely on a child-sized chair.
- The remaining children move around the police officer driving their 'cars'. When the police officer holds up the red 'traffic light' the cars will stop, and remain motionless, until the police officer holds up the green 'traffic light' to signal the drivers that they are allowed to move again. The game continues in this way.
- You could invite other children to play the role of the police officer as the game proceeds.

Variations

- Instead of driving cars, the children may enjoy motor bikes, tractors, trains, helicopters, space ships or even surfboards. Encourage children to come up with their own suggestions. Additionally, the children might like to enact ambulance or fire engine drama scenes as part of the game.
- Children in wheelchairs particularly enjoy this game.

Swinging

A rocking game

Age:	birth–2 years
Grouping:	individual
Resources:	none

How to play

◻ Hold the child in your arms. As you sing the song, rock the child to and fro; hold up high on 'now we go up' and lower to the floor on 'now we go down'. In general, older children enjoy more vigorous rocking than younger ones.

Variations

◻ This song is appropriate for play on a real swing with older children.

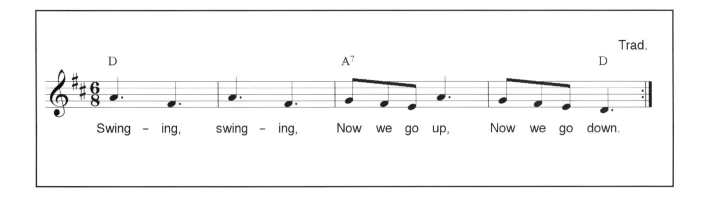

Trad.

Swing - ing, swing - ing, Now we go up, Now we go down.

Written by Veronicah Larkin and Louie Suthers

www.brilliantpublications.co.uk

Age:	birth–5 years
Grouping:	individual/small group
Resources:	none

Tap your shoulders

An action game

Tune: Frère Jacques

How to play

- ☐ Tickling game: hold baby on knee facing you and sing song. As you name each body part, touch, tap or tickle it according to the words of the song.

- ☐ Action game: older/more experience children will be able to do the actions themselves.

- ☐ Encourage children to invent alternative actions.

Note

For babies, this game is idea to incorporate into dressing and changing routines.

Toddlers will be able to join in the actions, tapping the named body parts, long before they can sing the song. However, as each line of the song is repeated, children who can sing, will learn it readily.

Tap your shoulders, tap your shoulders,
Touch your toes, touch your toes,
Tickle on your tummy, tickle on your tummy,
Where's your nose? There's your nose.

Tap your bottom, tap your bottom,
Touch your shin, touch your shin,
Tickle on your tickly feet, tickle on your tickly feet,
Where's your chin? There's your chin.

Teddy sing a song

A singing game

Tune: Row row row your boat

How to play

- Invite a child to hold Teddy, and jiggle him up and down as the children sing the song.
- When the song is finished, the child holding Teddy is encouraged to suggest a familiar song.
- The group then sings this song together, and Teddy is passed to another child who repeats the game.

Variations

- Often children who are familiar with this game will pretend that Teddy is whispering the name of the song to them.
- You might like to use alternatives to a teddy bear such as a rag doll, a cuddly toy or a puppet.

Age:	2–5 years
Grouping:	individual/small/medium/large group, children seated informally around adult
Resources:	a teddy bear

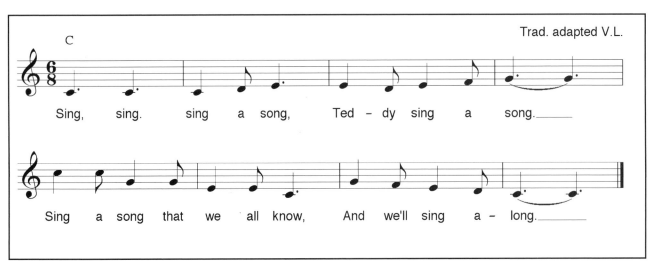

Trad. adapted V.L.

C

Sing, sing. sing a song, Ted - dy sing a song.____

Sing a song that we all know, And we'll sing a - long.____

Written by Veronicah Larkin and Louie Suthers
www.brilliantpublications.co.uk

The flying broomstick

A movement game

How to play

◘ Invite a child to straddle the broom and 'fly' around the inside of the circle, while the children sing a song, such as *There was an old witch.*

◘ When the song ends the child on the broom chooses a second child to join her/him on the broom, and the two children fly around the circle together while the remaining children sing the song again.

◘ At the end of the song the second child on the broom chooses a third child to join them on the broom, and so the game continues until no additional children can fit onto the broom.

Variations

◘ Some adults prefer to avoid the use of witches and witchcraft in songs and games for young children. The broom can be described, for example as, a car/plane/submarine/four-wheel drive, and an appropriate song or rhyme substituted such as *I'll take you riding in my car* or *The wheels on the bus.*

Age:	2–5 years
Grouping:	small/medium group, seated in a circle
Resources:	1 broom

The frog and the mosquitoes

A hoop game

Age:	3–5 years
Grouping:	small/medium/large group
Resources:	several hoops

How to play

- ☐ Depending on the size of the group, invite one or several children to play the role of the frog or frogs. Each frog is given a hoop which becomes a 'mosquito net'.
- ☐ The remaining children are the mosquitoes. You can encourage them to move around the room buzzing.
- ☐ Encourage the frogs to catch the mosquitoes by gently placing the hoop over them as they buzz around the space.
- ☐ Once mosquitoes are caught they are free to move around.

Variations

- ☐ If you desire, this game may be played in a competitive way. Once mosquitoes are caught they can withdraw from the game, or can become frogs and be given a hoop to try to catch the remaining mosquitoes. In this case, the final remaining mosquito is the winner.

Written by Veronicah Larkin and Louie Suthers
www.brilliantpublications.co.uk

Age:	4–5 years
Grouping:	medium/large group, open space suitable for movement
Resources:	recorded music

The long and the short of it

A line game

How to play

- ◘ Invite the children to look closely at the height of the other children in the group to compare with their own height.
- ◘ With your assistance, the children are encouraged to stand in a line, with the shortest child at one end and the tallest child at the other end.
- ◘ Remind the children to remember their position in the line.
- ◘ The children then move/dance around the space to the music.
- ◘ When the music stops the children are asked to return to their position in the line.

Variations

- ◘ Older/more experienced children sometimes enjoy the challenge of remembering their position over a period of time. You might like to play this game in the morning and then play it again in the afternoon, to see who has remembered their position.
- ◘ This game can be integrated with learning experiences related to children's growth/height charts. Children enjoy comparing their growth over time, so regular updating of the chart is important.

Written by Veronicah Larkin and Louie Suthers
www.brilliantpublications.co.uk

The old grey cat is sleeping

A movement game

Age:	3–5 years
Grouping:	small/medium/large group, large open space suitable for movement
Resources:	none

How to play

- One child is the cat, the rest of the group are mice.
- Sing the song and the children act out the story. Encourage the children to move and sing.

Variations

- Face paint, masks or costumes can make the dramatic play of this game even more fun.
- Children might like to devise a simple house using home corner equipment or a sheet draped over a low table.

1. The old grey cat is sleeping, sleeping, sleeping.
   The old grey cat is sleeping in the house.
2. The little mice come creeping, creeping, creeping.
   The little mice come creeping in the house.
3. The little mice are nibbling, nibbling, nibbling.
   The little mice are nibbling in the house.
4. The little mice are sleeping … in the house.
5. The old grey cat comes creeping … in the house.
6. The little mice all scamper … through the house.
7. The little mice are hiding … in the house.

Written by Veronicah Larkin and Louie Suthers
www.brilliantpublications.co.uk

Age:	3–5 years
Grouping:	small/medium/large group seated circle
Resources:	none

The up and down game

A listening game

How to play

- Invite a child to move into the middle of the circle and ask remaining children to close their eyes.
- The child in the middle chooses to either stand up or sit down on the floor.
- Once the position has been chosen the child makes a short statement, such as 'Good morning Blue Room.'
- Encourage the children in the circle to llisten carefully, and to decide whether the child in the middle is standing up or sitting down.

Variations

- The chosen statement might reinforce a particular concept, such as 'Today is Wednesday.'
- For older/more experienced children 3 positions may be chosen: standing up, sitting down and lying flat on the floor.

This is the way the ladies ride

A knee-bouncing game

Age:	6 months–2 years
Grouping:	individual, child on your knee
Resources:	none

How to play

- Say the rhyme and bounce the child. Each successive verse becomes more vigorous and is spoken more loudly.

- The child may want to face you; this provides a sense of security. Alternatively, the child may want to face away from you; this facilitates more energetic bouncing. Let the positioning in the game be guided by the temperament and mood of the child.

Variations

- If you have strong ankles, cross one leg over your knee and bounce the child on your foot.

- In the interest of anti-bias language, change the words to babies, children and teenagers. Alternatively, use the names of children in the group, with the child's own name for the last verse.

- Played with pushchairs, this game is also fun for non-mobile children. Start slowly, increasing the pace of the rhyme, with each verse.

Rhyme

This is the way the ladies ride
A-pace, a-pace, a-pace.
This is the way the gentlemen ride
Gallop, a-gallop, a-gallop.
And this is the way the farmers ride
Hobbledy-hoi! Hobbledy-hoi! Hobbledy-hoi!

Written by Veronicah Larkin and Louie Suthers
www.brilliantpublications.co.uk

This little cow

A tickling game

How to play

- Play with child on your lap or on the floor.
- This is a tickling game, which is very similar to *This little piggy* except that you start with the little toe.
- Say the rhyme, holding each toe in turn. On the 'And we'll chase … ' part, tickle up the child's leg and body to the chin, nose or neck.

Variations

- Use fingers instead of toes.

Rhyme

This little cow eats grass
This little cow eats hay
This little cow looks over the fence
And this little cow runs away
But this big cow does nothing at all but sleep in the sun all day
And we'll chase and we'll chase and we'll chase and we'll chase and we'll …

Three ropes in a circle

A rope game

Age:	3–5 years
Grouping:	small/medium group and 6 adults, large open space suitable for movement
Resources:	3 ropes (3–5 metres long depending upon the size of the group and the available playing space)

How to play

- ◻ You will need 6 adults or older children to hold the ends of the ropes.
- ◻ Place the ropes in the positions as indicated by the illustration and 6 segments will be formed.
- ◻ The ropes should be held parallel to the floor at a height of approximately 30 cms. (This is just a guide as the distance will be dictated by the size/height of the children playing).
- ◻ Invite the children to crawl, slither and wriggle under the ropes, moving in a roughly circular fashion.
- ◻ Encourage the children to stay close to the floor to avoid touching the ropes.
- ◻ Children might like to move around on their backs or on their tummies.
- ◻ Continue to play the game while the children remain interested.

Variations

- ◻ You may begin the game with the ropes at a higher distance from the floor, and then gradually decrease the distance as children's skills increase.
- ◻ A useful variation is to invite children to step/ jump over the ropes, moving in a roughly circular fashion, or to alternate between moving over one rope and then crawling under the next.
- ◻ Brightly coloured ropes are available from many hardware suppliers.

Written by Veronicah Larkin and Louie Suthers
www.brilliantpublications.co.uk

Age: 6 months–2 years
Grouping: individual, child can be sitting on a change table, in a bath, or on your lap
Resources: a scarf, a flannel (a hat or a length of soft fabric can be used too)

Tom tom tiddly

A lap game

How to play

- Gently place the scarf over/near to the child's face.
- As you say the rhyme reveal a little more of the child's face until the whole face is uncovered.
- Repeat while child remains interested.

Variations

- Some young children do not enjoy the sensation of having their face covered, so you could hold the scarf near (but not touching) the face.
- A sheer scarf will assist the child to see you throughout the game.
- Sometimes the child will attempt to take the scarf from you and cover your face while you say the rhyme.

Rhyme

Tom, tom, tiddly tin
I can see Rosa's chin,
Tom, tom, tiddly touth
I can see Rosa's mouth,
Tom, tom, tiddly toes
I can see Rosa's nose,
Tom, tom, tiddly ties
I can see Rosa's eyes,
Tom, tom, tiddly tair
I can see Rosa's hair,
Tom, tom, tiddly tears
I can see Rosa's ears,
Tom, tom, tiddly ted
I can see Rosa's head,
Tom, tom, tiddly tow
I can see Rosa now!

Substitute child's name here.

Two little dickie birds

A drama game

Age:	2–5 years
Grouping:	small/medium group, seated informally around an adult
Resources:	child-sized table or similar (optional)

How to play

- ☐ Acquaint the children with the rhyme Two little dickie birds.
- ☐ Invite one child to play 'Peter' and another to play 'Paul' then assist them to enact the rhyme.
- ☐ The wall in the rhyme could be represented by a child sized table or bench, for instance.
- ☐ The game continues with interested children taking the roles of 'Peter' and 'Paul'.

Variations

- ☐ Once children are familiar with the game you could invent your own words. Some examples might be: 2 little green frogs (hop away), 2 little pilots (fly away), 2 little trainers (jog away) and 2 little racing cars (zoom away).
- ☐ In the interests of developing an anti-bias curriculum, you could use female names and names from a variety of cultures. Additionally, you could use the children's own names.
- ☐ You might like to add dramatic play props from the dressing-up box for a different dimension to the game. You could invite children to choose a character and they could dress accordingly.

Rhyme

Two little dickie birds sitting on a wall
One named Peter and one named Paul
Fly away Peter, fly away Paul
Come back Peter, come back Paul.

Written by Veronicah Larkin and Louie Suthers
www.brilliantpublications.co.uk

Age:	20 months–5 years
Grouping:	individual/small/medium/large group
Resources:	none

Two naughty monkeys

An action game

How to play

◻ Say rhyme and do actions. Toddlers will join in with the actions before they can say the rhyme. They will gradually pick up some of the words.

Variations

◻ Play the game as a jumping chant on a mini-trampoline.

◻ 2-and-3 year-olds will enjoy dramatizing the rhyme, doing appropriate movements for each line. With children of this age there will be no allocation of roles. All the children playing will enact the rhyme. In effect, the finger play becomes a rhyme with whole body movements.

◻ Older children like to increase the number of monkeys (3, 4 or 5 work well) and subtract one each time. They are also ready to take on specific roles, for example 5 monkeys, Mumma and the doctor.

◻ Children may enjoy using dressing-up clothes and props, such as a telephone or doctor's bag, to extend this dramatic play.

Rhyme

Two naughty monkeys jumping on the bed
One fell down and hurt her/his head
Mummy called the doctor and the doctor said
'No more monkeys jumping on the bed!'

Move 2 index fingers up and down.
One finger to the floor then hold the head.
Phoning actions.
Wag index finger authoritatively.

Written by Veronicah Larkin and Louie Suthers
www.brilliantpublications.co.uk

Under and over

A rope game

Age:	2–5 years
Grouping:	individual/small/medium group, large open space suitable for movement
Resources:	2 lengths of rope (approximately 3 metres)

How to play

- Both ropes are held parallel to each other by adults or older children.
- Invite the children to crawl under the first rope and then jump/step over the second. The ropes should be held at a comfortable distance from the floor to enable children to move freely and safely.
- Encourage children to repeat the movements or invent their own ways of moving under and over the 2 ropes.

Variations

- There are a wide variety of rope games suitable for young children.
- Additional ropes may be added so children can move under/over/under/over in succession.
- Another variation is to invite children to sit in a circle on the floor and hold several ropes across the circle. Children can then move under and over the ropes in a circular way.
- Some rope games require a large open area and may be more suited to playing in an outdoor environment.
- Rope games can be successfully played in the garden or local park as well.

What will we play today?

Written by Veronicah Larkin and Louie Suthers
www.brilliantpublications.co.uk

Wake up Santa

A singing game
Tune: Frère Jacques

Age:	2–5 years
Grouping:	individual/small/medium/large group, children gathered informally around an adult
Resources:	none

How to play
◻ Sing the song and do the actions as indicated.
◻ Repeat as often as children's interest is maintained.

Variations
◻ Children can gather in a circle with a child as 'sleeping Santa' in the middle. The children can sing the song and attempt to wake Santa.

Trad. adapted V.L.

San – ta's snor – ing, San – ta's snor – ing, Not a peep, Not a peep,

San – ta's snor – ing, San – ta's snor – ing, He's a – sleep, He's a – sleep.

Santa's snoring,   *Child pretends to sleep and*
Santa's snoring,   *makes loud snoring noises.*
Not a peep,
Not a peep,
Santa's snoring,
Santa's snoring,
He's asleep,
He's asleep.
Shake him, shake him,   *Child begins to stir.*
Shake him, shake him,
Wake up now,
Wake up now,
Now it's nearly Christmas,
Now it's nearly Christmas,
Stay awake,   *Child wakes up.*
Stay awake!

Wake up you sleepy heads

A singing game

Age:	20 months–4 years
Grouping:	small/medium group, younger children can play this game gathered around an adult; older or more experienced children can use a circle formation
Resources:	bell or shaker for signal sound; a toy that makes a mooing sound can be fun for the children

How to play

- ◘ Begin with everyone standing up. Sing the first (fast) part of the song 'Wake up you sleepy heads … ' and jump up and down. Pause when you reach 'cows'.
- ◘ Then sing the second (slow) part of the song.
- ◘ Gradually kneel down, then lie down on the floor/ground. Pretend to sleep, include deep breathing and snoring.
- ◘ Continue to 'sleep' until the signal (bell/shaker/mooing sound), then everyone quickly jumps up.
- ◘ Repeat game as required, finishing at the end of the first section.

Variations

- ◘ Let a child play the getting up signal.
- ◘ For older/more experienced children the game works well as dramatic play with groups of farmers and cows.

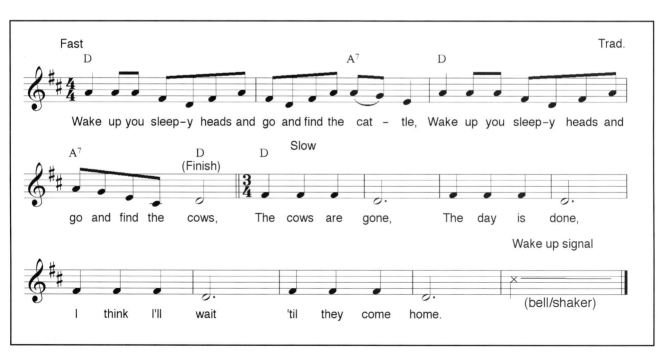

Written by Veronicah Larkin and Louie Suthers
www.brilliantpublications.co.uk

Age:	2–5 years
Grouping:	individual/small/medium group
Resources:	masking tape

Walk the plank
A movement game

How to play

- ☐ Apply a length of masking tape to the floor in a long straight line.
- ☐ Encourage the children to walk carefully along the line.
- ☐ As the first child is nearing the end of the line, the second child can begin.
- ☐ Continue to play in this manner while children's interest is maintained.

Variations

- ☐ As an alternative to masking tape you can draw a line on carpet or wood with white chalk. This rubs off easily at the end of the game.
- ☐ You could provide additional challenges, such as children balancing a small bean bag on their head as they walk the line, or clapping hands/tapping shoulders/nodding heads as they walk.
- ☐ Another way to extend the game for older/ more experienced children is by substituting jumping/hopping/skipping for walking, or by asking the children to walk backwards along the line.
- ☐ You could encourage children to make up a pirate story or other dramatic role play games.
- ☐ This game may be played successfully along pathways/outdoors.

Written by Veronicah Larkin and Louie Suthers
www.brilliantpublications.co.uk

Wet washing

A drama game

Age:	2–5 years
Grouping:	small/medium group large open space suitable for movement
Resources:	a length of rope

How to play

- A length of rope is stretched out, held at a young child's shoulder or head height by 2 adults. This is the clothes line.
- Invite a child to take on the role of Mrs Wishy Washy. Encourage the child to choose individual children to 'hang up on the washing line'.
- Mrs Wishy Washy decides what type of garment each child is, and hangs them up accordingly.
- Invite another child to take on the role of the 'wind' and encourage that child to blow the washing so that all the children move in the breeze.
- The song Wet washing hanging on the line may be sung during this game.

Variations

- The stories Mrs Mopple's washing day and Mrs Wishy Washy may be good starting points or follow-ups for this game.

Written by Veronicah Larkin and Louie Suthers
www.brilliantpublications.co.uk

Age:	3–5 years
Grouping:	small/medium/large group, seated in a circle
Resources:	blindfold/scarf (optional)

What am I wearing?
A work-it-out game

How to play

◻ Invite a child to come into the middle of the circle with closed eyes or wearing a blindfold.

◻ Describe the clothing of a child in the group, for example 'This child is wearing a green top, red shorts and blue shoes.' The child in the middle of the circle is encouraged to identify the child whose clothing has been described.

◻ Once the child has been identified, you can invite new children to be the 'identifier' and the 'described'.

Variations

◻ It's important to keep in mind that some young children do not like the sensation of being blindfolded. The game can be played successfully by encouraging children to close their eyes. The game can be made more challenging by describing only one article of clothing.

◻ Another variation is to invite a child to describe the clothing of another child.

What does the baby say?

A following game

Age: 12–24 months
Grouping: individual/small group
Resources: none

How to play

- An adult says the rhyme below, pausing at the points where the children can make the sounds (marked **).
- At first you will probably need to say the whole rhyme, but once the children become familiar with the game they will join in. Don't be concerned if the child only says one 'ma' or 'moo' – that's great!

Variations

- Adapt the rhyme to whatever sounds the child can make: what does the cat/car/horse say?
- Use the pictures in a book as the stimulus for the game. It works well with animal books.
- Use animal hand or finger puppets or soft toys as props for the game.
- Older children often join in with both lines of animal sounds once they know the pattern.

Rhyme

1. What does the baby say?
   Ma, ma, ma.
   Say what the baby says
   ** Ma, ma, ma.

2. What does the dog say?
   Woof, woof, woof.
   Say what the dog says
   ** Woof, woof, woof.

3. What does the cow say?
   Moo, moo, moo.
   Say what the cow says
   ** Moo, moo, moo.

4. What does your mummy/daddy/adult's own name say?
   I love you or X X X (kissing sounds)
   Say what the mummy/daddy/adult says
   ** I love you or X X X.

Written by Veronicah Larkin and Louie Suthers
www.brilliantpublications.co.uk

Age:	2–5 years
Grouping:	individual/small/large group, gathered around an adult or in a circle
Resources:	none

What will we play today?

A movement game

How to play

- Everyone sings the chorus and claps hands or 'pats' knees.
- One child suggests an action or movement.
- Everyone does their version of the nominated movement and sings the verse. The words change every verse to match the chosen movement.
- Repeat the chorus, and another child selects an action. The game continues in this manner until all interested children have had a turn – or everyone is exhausted!

Variations

- Limit the actions to movements you do sitting down or standing in your spot.
- Play it as a stick game.
- Combine two actions such as clap and hop.
- Challenge the children to sing as well as doing the actions, otherwise, you'll find that you're the only one singing.

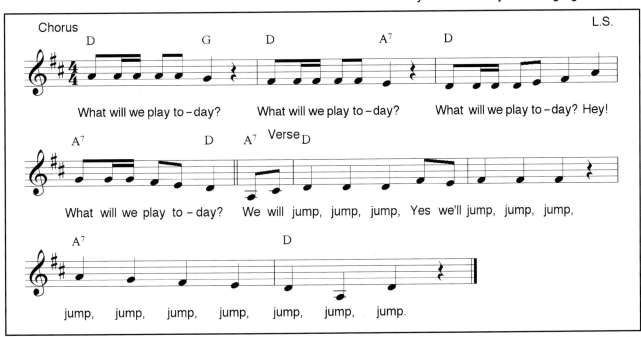

Written by Veronicah Larkin and Louie Suthers

www.brilliantpublications.co.uk

What's in a name?

A listening game

Age:	4–5 years
Grouping:	small/medium/large group, a large open space suitable for movement
Resources:	a name card for each child in the group, and a set of simple percussion instruments/sound makers

How to play

- ◘ Place the name cards at intervals around the room on the floor.
- ◘ Invite a number of children to play the instruments while the remaining children move/dance around the room.
- ◘ When the music stops encourage the children to find their name cards. The game can be repeated many times, with new children playing in the 'band/orchestra' while the name cards are moved to different positions around the room.

Variations

- ◘ Many name card games are successful with older/more experienced children. Name cards can be placed on beds or lunch tables, and children can find their bed/table place in this manner.
- ◘ Additionally, children could make their own name card place mats to use throughout the year. If laminated, these mats will resist moisture and staining.

Written by Veronicah Larkin and Louie Suthers

www.brilliantpublications.co.uk

Age:	2–5 years
Grouping:	small/large group, seated informally around an adult or in a circle
Resources:	a pair of sticks for each player

When I was one
A stick game

How to play

❏ Sing song and tap sticks to the beat as appropriate for lyrics. Younger children will probably do the actions only, but older ones will sing along as they use their sticks.

Variations

❏ Children may like to add extra verses, inventing new words and actions.

❏ Adults or children can invent special ways of putting down the sticks at the end of the song, for example

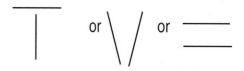

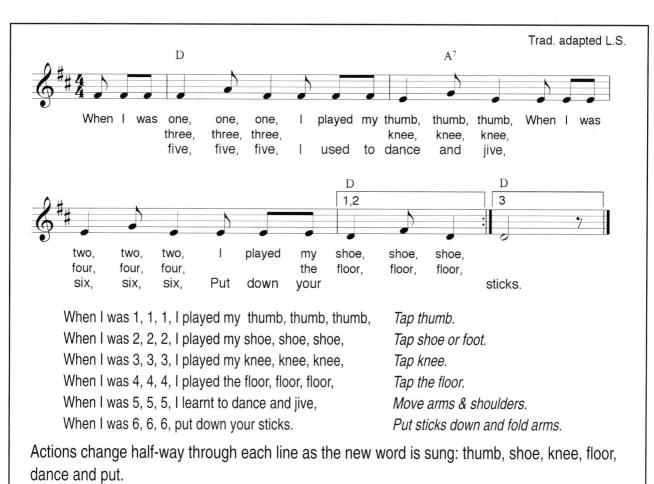

When I was 1, 1, 1, I played my thumb, thumb, thumb,   *Tap thumb.*
When I was 2, 2, 2, I played my shoe, shoe, shoe,   *Tap shoe or foot.*
When I was 3, 3, 3, I played my knee, knee, knee,   *Tap knee.*
When I was 4, 4, 4, I played the floor, floor, floor,   *Tap the floor.*
When I was 5, 5, 5, I learnt to dance and jive,   *Move arms & shoulders.*
When I was 6, 6, 6, put down your sticks.   *Put sticks down and fold arms.*

Actions change half-way through each line as the new word is sung: thumb, shoe, knee, floor, dance and put.

Written by Veronicah Larkin and Louie Suthers
www.brilliantpublications.co.uk

When the music stops

A listening game

Age:	2–5 years
Grouping:	individual/small/medium/large group, large open space suitable for movement
Resources:	recorded music

How to play

- Invite the children to move/dance around the space while the music is playing.
- When the music stops encourage the children to adopt a frozen position and to remain in that position until the music starts again.
- Continue to play while children's interest is maintained.

Variations

- You can use a variety of different music. Encourage children to listen carefully, and to interpret the music in their own way as they move around the space.
- When the music stops the children could take on the frozen shape of a favourite animal.
- Children could run into a designated space when the music stops, sit, or crouch down on the floor.
- Encourage mobility-challenged children to find their own unique way to reflect the music.
- Ask children to make suggestions of what they would like to do when the music stops.

Written by Veronicah Larkin and Louie Suthers

www.brilliantpublications.co.uk

Age:	2–5 years
Grouping:	small/medium/large group, seated in a circle
Resources:	Santa Claus hat

Where is Santa ?

A singing game
Tune: Clementine

How to play

◘ Encourage the children to close their eyes as they sing the first 3 lines of the song.

◘ Invite a child to skip around the outside of the circle as the song is sung, and place the Santa Claus hat behind a child.

◘ On the line 'Can we find him?' children reach behind them to see if the hat is there.

◘ The child who finds the hat puts it on while the group sings 'We have found you Santa Claus.'

◘ Repeat the game, inviting new children to hide the hat.

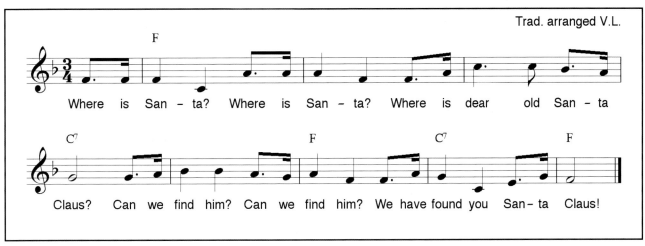

Trad. arranged V.L.

Where is San - ta? Where is San - ta? Where is dear old San - ta Claus? Can we find him? Can we find him? We have found you San - ta Claus!

Where's the music?

A listening game

How to play

- Adult turns on the music box/toy and hides it. The child or children find the music box/toy.
- With babies and young toddlers, 'the music' can be hidden very obviously under a cushion or a plastic ice cream container.
- Older toddlers enjoy the ritual of hiding their eyes (although hardly any do) then finding 'the music'.

Variations

- Older toddlers can play this game seated informally on a mat. All children cover their eyes, and one is given 'the music' to hide in the children's laps or under their jumpers. The children then open their eyes and listen for 'who has the music'.
- 2-and-3-year-olds can play a more challenging version of the game, where all the children cover their eyes and one child hides the music in the room. When they open their eyes the others search for it.

Age:	9 months–3 years
Grouping:	individual/small/medium group children gathered informally around an adult
Resources:	music box or other toy that plays music

Written by Veronicah Larkin and Louie Suthers
www.brilliantpublications.co.uk

Which one am I going to play?

A listening game
Tune: Shortnin' Bread

Age: 3–5 years

Grouping: individual/small/medium group, gathered informally around an adult or in a circle

Resources: a variety of instruments, toys or other objects that can produce a sound

How to play

- Play each of the sound makers in turn to familiarize the children with their sounds. Initially use 3 or 4 instruments.
- Everyone sings the song and covers their eyes. One child, previously chosen, makes a sound on one of the instruments.
- The others open their eyes when asked to 'wake up'. In turn they attempt to reproduce the sound they heard by making a sound with one of the sound makers.
- Repeat this step until everyone agrees that the sound has been found.
- Play the game again, letting another child have a turn at making the sound. Continue as required.

Variations

- Depending on the age and language development of the children, instead of reproducing the sound, they can identify its source by naming the instrument or touching it.
- The game becomes more challenging if the number of sound makers is increased.
- If the children are very experienced, two sounds, either one after the other or together, can be used. Identifying two sounds requires careful listening.

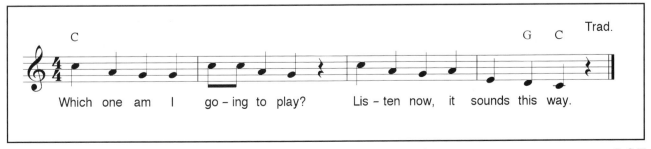

Which one am I go-ing to play? Lis-ten now, it sounds this way.

Who rang the bell?

A listening game

Age:	2–5 years
Grouping:	small/medium/large group, seated in a circle
Resources:	a bell

How to play

- Invite a child to sit in the middle of the circle with eyes closed.
- Move quietly around the outside of the circle and give the bell to a child.
- The child rings the bell loudly and then places it behind her/him.
- The child in the middle of the circle is encouraged to open her/his eyes and to identify who was ringing the bell.
- The game continues with a new child in the middle of the circle and a new child ringing the bell.

Variations

- A variety of musical instruments/sound makers can be substituted for the bell.
- Alternatively, you could ask children to clap their hands several times, in place of the bell.
- For a child with impaired motor skills, who has difficulty holding or ringing a conventional bell, you could make a simple 'bell bracelet' by attaching small light-weight bells on a length of ribbon and securing this around the child's wrist.
- This game can be adapted for Christmas, by using a sleigh bell and referring to the child in the middle as 'Santa Claus trying to find his reindeer'.

Written by Veronicah Larkin and Louie Suthers

www.brilliantpublications.co.uk

Age:	3–5 years
Grouping:	small/medium group, seated informally around an adult
Resources:	none

Who's behind me?

A listening game

How to play

- Choose a child to stand up, facing away from the remaining children who are seated.

- Invite a child from the group to make a short statement, such as 'I can see Thomas at pre-school today.'

- The child who is facing away from the group attempts to identify the speaker. If identification is difficult, the speaker could make a longer statement, such as 'Well Thomas, I like to play in the sand pit and the home corner ... '

- Once the speaker is identified you can invite new children to be the 'speaker' and the 'identifier'.

Variations

- For children who are familiar with the voices of the group, the game can be more challenging by encouraging children to offer a short statement, such as 'Hello', or by communicating to the child by using a 'funny voice'.

Written by Veronicah Larkin and Louie Suthers

www.brilliantpublications.co.uk

Who's under the blanket?

A work-it-out game

Age:	2–5 years
Grouping:	small/medium group
Resources:	a blanket or sheet large enough to comfortably cover a crouching child

How to play

- ☐ Invite children to find a space in the room and to crouch down into a small ball with eyes closed.
- ☐ Choose a child and gently place the blanket over the child.
- ☐ Invite the remaining children to 'wake up' and identify who is under the blanket.
- ☐ Once the covered child has been identified, remove the blanket and invite children to find a new space in the room.
- ☐ When all the children are crouching down again, choose a new child to cover with the blanket.
- ☐ The game continues in this manner.

Variations

- ☐ If the children have difficulty identifying the covered child, you could gradually uncover parts of the child, such as the child's shoes, while asking, 'Who is wearing yellow trainers today?'
- ☐ You might like to choose a section of music with several distinct changes throughout. Children can be encouraged to move/dance to the music, and when they hear the music change they can assume the crouching position.
- ☐ Once children are familiar with the game you can invite them to take turns covering another child in the group.

Written by Veronicah Larkin and Louie Suthers

www.brilliantpublications.co.uk

Age:	2–5 years
Grouping:	small/medium/large group, seated informally
Resources:	screen/large sheet

Whose shoes?

A work-it-out game

How to play

- ◘ Invite children to find a place on the mat and sit with their eyes closed.
- ◘ Move around the mat and choose 3 or 4 children to stand up and move behind the screen. The children should stand or sit so that only their shoes are visible to the children remaining on the mat.
- ◘ Encourage the group to open their eyes, and to identify the children behind the screen by their shoes.
- ◘ Continue to play while interest is maintained.

Variations

- ◘ You could substitute a large sheet for the screen. The chosen children are invited to sit on the floor with their legs stretched out in front of them. Place the sheet over them, leaving their shoes exposed.
- ◘ Variations on shoes might include bare feet, hands, sections of hair, or the back of the head.

Written by Veronicah Larkin and Louie Suthers
www.brilliantpublications.co.uk

Yal satarim

A singing game

Age:	4–5 years
Grouping:	small/medium/large group, seated in a circle
Resources:	small bean bag

How to play

- ☐ Everyone sings the song and claps.
- ☐ One child walks around the outside of the circle, carrying the oil and honey (bean bag) and places it behind a child.
- ☐ When the seated child realizes that she/he has been given the oil and honey, the child jumps up and chases the oil and honey vendor around the circle until the vendor is caught, or reaches the vacant place in the circle.
- ☐ Repeat as many times as required.

Note

As the song is repeated many times during the game, the children will have no trouble in 'catching' the words. Don't worry about trying to teach them the words separately.

The words of the song mean 'I am selling oil. I am selling honey.' Note that 'Ustam' is pronounced 'oostam'.

Trad. Turkish

Yal sat–ar–im, Bal sat–ar–im, Us–tam yok–tur, Ben sat–ar–im.

Rhyme
Yal satarim,
Bal satarim,
Ustam yoktur,
Ben satarim.

Written by Veronicah Larkin and Louie Suthers

www.brilliantpublications.co.uk

Acknowledgements

The authors acknowledge the generous grant provided by the Institute of Early Childhood, Macquarie University, which enabled them to undertake extensive trialling of the games in early childhood settings.

The photographs appearing throughout the book were taken at Gumnut Cottage, Macquarie University. We thank the families, staff and children for their co-operation.

In addition, the authors are indebted to the patience and good humour of the families, staff and children of Paddington Eastside Child Care Centre, in particular Fran Hughes, Rebecca Lawson and Liz Woolford whose constructive and honest feedback was greatly appreciated.

Brilliant Publications have at present over 80 books in their range, starting with several series covering art, games and stories for the early years, through to a flexible range of photocopiable books linked to the National Curriculum Key Stages 1 and 2. Brilliant Publications also produce several series of books which are designed specifically to give extra support to pupils with learning difficulties, however these books can also be used to boost younger pupils who are specially gifted.

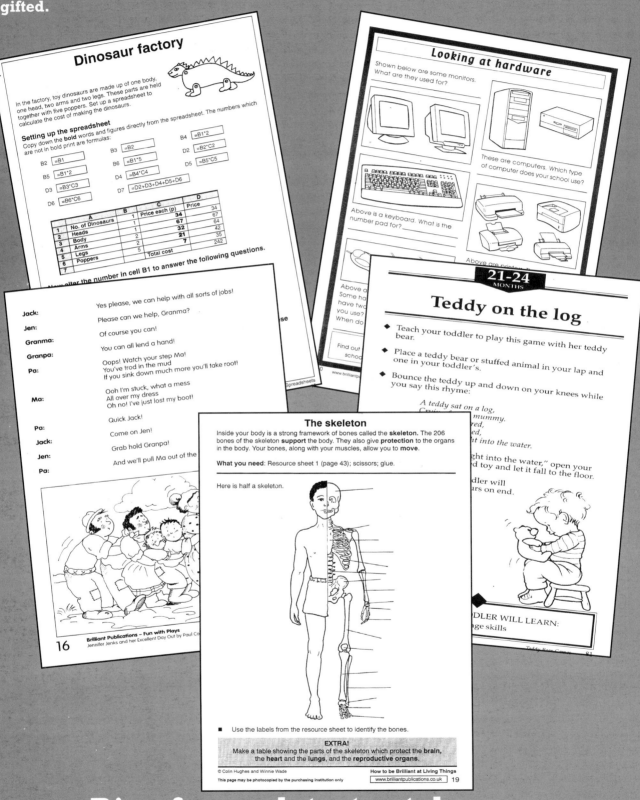